The Infinite Universe

by

Robert Allan Stewart

FALCON PRESS
LAS VEGAS, NEVADA

International Standard Book Number: 0-941404-98-6

First edition – 1989
Published by Falcon Press

Typography by Royal Type
27 West 20th Street • Room 1005
New York, NY 10011

Cover Painting by Jane Nelson
Cover Design by Studio 31

FALCON PRESS
1209 South Casino Center, Suite 147
Las Vegas, Nevada 89104
1-800-545-3266 • 1-702-385-5749

Manufactured in the United States of America

Contents

FURTHER CONSPIRACIES?!

If you would like to read further on the New Age Conspiracy to elevate Human Consciousness on this Planet and elsewhere—don't simply ask your book dealer to order the following titles—Demand that S/He do so! They are:

THE FUTURE HISTORY SERIES
By Timothy Leary, Ph.D.

Info-Psychology
Neuropolitique
The Intelligence Agents
What Does WoMan Want?
Millennium Madness
The Game Of Life

THE ROBERT ANTON WILSON SERIES

The Cosmic Trigger
Sex and Drugs
Wilhelm Reich In Hell
Prometheus Rising
Coincidance—A New Anthology
Ishtar Rising: Book of the Breast

THE FUTURE IS *NOW* SERIES

Undoing Yourself With Energized Meditation and Other Devices • By Christopher S. Hyatt, Ph.D., Introduced by Israel Regardie, Extensive Foreword by Robert Anton Wilson.
A Modern Shaman's Guide to a Pregnant Universe • by C.S. Hyatt, Ph.D. & Antero Alli
Breaking The GodSpell: Genetic Evolution • by Neil Freer, Introduced by Zecharia Sitchin.
The Sapiens System—The Illuminati Conspiracy: Their Objectives, Methods & Who They Are! • By Donald Holmes, M.D., Extensive Introduction by Robert Anton Wilson.
Angel Tech: A Modern Shaman's Guide to Reality Selection • by Antero Alli, Preface by Robert Anton Wilson.
All Rites Reversed?!: Ritual Technology for Self-Initiation • by Antero Alli
Zen Without Zen Masters • by Camden Benares.
Monsters and Magical Sticks: There Is No Such Thing As Hypnosis? • By Steven Heller, Ph.D., Introduced by Robert Anton Wilson
The Cybernetic Conspiracy (Mind Over Matter) • by Constantin Negoita, Ph.D.
An Extraterrestrial Conspiracy • by Marian Greenberg
The Shaman Warrior • by Gini Graham Scott, Ph.D.
A Search for Meaning: Towards a Psychology of Fulfillment • by Alan Garner
Power and Empowerment • by Lynn Atkinson, Ph.D.
The Dream Illuminati Vimana Conspiracy • by Wayne Saalman, Introduced by Robert Anton Wilson
Mega-Babies: Baby Boomers are Booming • by Timothy Leary, Ph.D., C.S. Hyatt, Ph.D., & Linda Miller, R.N., B.S.N.
Angelettes and Cosmic Sex • by Pusser
RX Shiksa • by J.R. Ephraim
Blue Star • by Bonnie Hadley

Don't forget **THE JUNGIAN PSYCHOLOGY SERIES**
THE GOLDEN DAWN SERIES • THE ALEISTER CROWLEY SERIES

For a free catalog of all Falcon titles contact:

FALCON PRESS

1209 South Casino Center, Suite 147 • Las Vegas, NV 89104
U.S.A. 800-545-3266 or 702-385-5749

FOREWORD

This book is based on channeled information. By "channeled", I mean communications with entities who do not live on our physical plane. These entities are souls much like us. At a time when the existence of even the human soul is in doubt, many of my readers may not find this assertion credible. Many may even find it threatening. Certainly, Western societies frown upon any serious consideration of life beyond terrestrial earth, especially life that involves the survival of the human soul or nonhuman guides. Nonetheless, I stand behind my claim.

In a sense, I am a medium. I do not possess a high degree of psychic ability, but my experience has proved you do not need to be highly psychic to benefit from channeled information. In all respects, I am a very ordinary person with an ordinary set of talents. For reasons I don't fully understand, I have been selected to convey certain ideas that originate from beyond my known self and world. This source, though still largely a mystery to me, provides evidence for man's traditional religious and mythological beliefs in gods and other unseen life. My work, then, is largely aimed at secularizing an integral human quest in terms modern secular societies are comfortable with.

I was led to this work by certain experiences that do not fit an everyday mold. These experiences, such as precognition, mediumship, and psychokinesis, are as real as any of my other day-to-day experiences. They are a part of my life I can't ignore, even if I wanted to. Through my exploration of human mysteries and mysticism, I have found my life enriched in many ways. Most of all I have the satisfaction of knowing how I fit into not just the world of the biological organism, but also the world of the soul.

I have used and developed techniques that are traditionally viewed as mystical. I believe this traditional regard is somewhat misplaced. The mysticism of my techniques (most of them used by many other people past and present) lies mainly in the fact that science has to date given little effort to exploring them seriously, preferring instead more tangible pursuits. That's fair, but I think scientists (and therefore humanity in general) have consequently missed out on some very exciting discoveries.

One such discovery is that man is not alone in his quest for knowledge. There are other intelligent entities within the framework of this planet. We have known of their existence for centuries; typically, we have called them gods. In our awe, we have failed to approach our gods in a manner consistent with scientific investigation.

Science, seeking to distance its investigations from what are perceived to be superstitious beliefs, has carefully avoided any direct investigation of divine powers. This has resulted in an unbalanced understanding of the nature of our planet and our universe. This book is one more step in the process of defining a context in which such investigation may someday occur.

This is my second book. The first, *Man's Unending Quest*, is also based on channeled information. It describes the soul as a physical entity, and its cycles of reincarnation. It also introduces the Guides of Man, entities which have long guided human affairs. These guides are often taken to be gods or God, depending on the point of view of the person contacted. They are kind, patient and loving, and each one of us has specific guides of our own. My own guides have assisted me in this writing; in fact, they have enlisted me as a vehicle through which they present their ideas. I attempt to do so in a manner which is reasonable, coherent, and readable. Through me, my guides hope to explain portions of the human experience that too often escape our notice while we live in this world.

In time, these ideas will be fully tested. Meanwhile, there is much to be gained from using channeled information in our daily lives. It can help us gain the confidence we need to conquer life's hurdles. It provides a vital context: the knowledge of who and what we are, and where we are going; it can even give us a sense of belonging. At a time when industrialized civilizations easily lose their community of spirit, it is nice to know there are familiar networks to draw upon.

R.A.S.

INTRODUCTION

This book is an exploration of the human soul and its place in an infinite universe. The universe has no fixed limits, even though there are many limitations for everything that exists within it. As a part of the universe, each one of us struggles with personal limitations: we are limited by our abilities, our physical construction and the very environment that sustains us.

We are more dependent on our environment than we habitually notice. Environment is everything that we are not; it is the whole universe. However, the universe is so immense that we cannot hope to understand it all. For practicality's sake we must think in terms of a working environment—the physical forces and conditions around us that have the greatest impact on our lives.

It is easy to think of environment as just the immediate biological ecosystems of this world. Such is our natural perception as biological organisms. But environment goes beyond any one world, no matter how complex and vital that world may be. Our environment extends into outer space: this planet is only one planet in a solar system, our solar system only one solar system in a galaxy, and our galaxy only one galaxy in the cosmos.

Each material body in the cosmos has some effect on our planet and therefore our lives. The sun by far has the greatest impact; the moon and other planets have lesser influences but affect our world—and us—to some degree through their gravitational fields. Even the farthest star systems have slight effects on us. Their light travels across billions of light-years of space to reach us, thereby interacting directly with our world. More, they are part of the self-defining order of the cosmos. Each body, however remote or insubstantial, has some effect in establishing the overall organization of the cosmos.

Our environment extends even beyond the cosmos. There are other levels of physical reality that affect our world (and our lives) to a degree not so great as, say, the sun, but far more than remote galaxies. These other levels of reality exist parallel to the material cosmos. Alternate worlds act within the same space our terrestrial earth occupies. Normally we don't perceive these alternate or parallel worlds, but we know of them through the mysticism and religions of every human culture.

Science has often postulated the existence of parallel worlds. On what terms these worlds exist is subject to much speculation. At times it is difficult to separate serious speculation from science fiction, but

3

both use ever-active human imagination as a stimulus. Even so, imagination is not to be discounted. It is a valuable tool for envisioning realities that are not yet discovered in empirical terms—as is evidenced by the novels of moon flights written by H.G. Wells, Edgar Rice Burroughs, and others decades before such flight was believed possible.

It is clear through a survey of man's myths, legends, and beliefs (both ancient and modern) that in some deeper aspect of our consciousness we accept the notion of alternate or parallel worlds. These worlds influence ours, and influence us as individuals. More than just the fancy of precocious writers, these alternate realities attempt to touch us through the lower levels of our consciousness. Consciousness is a far more powerful tool of perception and control of environment than we think.

We can use our individual consciousness to explore these other worlds. When we do, we find them to be liberally populated. We can learn first-hand of the myriad entities that have sparked our most venerable legends and myths. We can meet some of these entities on their own terms, and begin to understand how and why they have stimulated man through the ages to seek higher truths. Such contact can be achieved many ways, including mediumship and the projection of consciousness out of the organic body known as astral projection. These are techniques that I have used, but such techniques are not always necessary; many people achieve satisfactory contact through meditation or prayer.

Regardless of our personal beliefs, we all have relationships with other worlds through our base levels of consciousness. This internal contact is constant, consistent, and very integral to our being. Unfortunately, many of us only achieve an awareness of the nonterrestrial worlds of our planet after the death of the organic body. The realization then is usually swift, but does little to alter the perceptions of those who are left behind. Not much can be done to convince people who do not believe in the survival of the soul that there are indeed worlds beyond this one. But believers or not, we all join another world when we die.

Each one of us has experienced death many times. Death, like birth, is an awakening. Each transition is a refocusing of the total consciousness on an alternate working environment. While in flesh, we view our environment primarily through the organic senses. Out of flesh, we view it differently. The discarnate soul perceives its environment via abilities we often describe as extrasensory perception, or ESP. This perception is not limited to the discarnate soul. Anyone can develop such ESP skills as telepathy, clairvoyance, and precognition. Unfortunately, our mental control of these skills while in flesh is quite limited.

For the most part, mankind has two primary working environments. One is this world, which we can call terrestrial earth. The other is the Afterlife. Both environments impose limitations on the individual. In terms of our terrestrial existence, our most critical limitation is an inability or unwillingness to view the universe as an open system.

Many of us view the cosmos as being the complete universe, a closed system as defined in Einsteinian physics. Although that perception does not harm us, it does limit us. Such a limitation is analogous to a deer that is only aware of the meadow in which it is browsing. The awareness of environment is focused on what seems important at the time and does not look beyond the immediate sensory enclave. For the deer such as awareness is sufficient. The deer doesn't require an understanding of its environment; it is content with a place to live.

Unlike the deer, we seek a greater definition of our environment. We wish to understand it as well as experience it. Our motives are to some extent as simple as the deer's, as we use our knowledge to enhance our survival. At the same time, we improve the quality of our lives, satisfy our curiosity, and pursue knowledge for learning's sake.

But even with such enhanced desires, the usual modern perception is that environment is just a more or less stable set of organic, geological and meteorological conditions. We often don't recognize that there is much more to our environment that meets our eyes, a limitation that results from our focus on sensory perceptions. These perceptions have been tuned through biological evolution to aid our corporeal survival; in the process, we have allowed some of our special extrasensory skills to decline. Although this trend may not be detrimental to our survival, is it necessary? Why lose skills that can enhance our lives if we don't have to? I believe we can reverse the trend if we so choose, and derive great benefits from doing so. If we care to do so, it is up to us to act. We may even find that developing our psychic skills will give us an edge in the game of survival.

To the universe, the human race is just another physical pattern that may or may not continue for an indefinite period. The universe, as a physical entity, does not care if humanity survives or perishes. But to us, survival is of great and immediate concern. Although our species will certainly become extinct some day, just as every other species will someday be extinct, there is no reason why that extinction has to be soon. With more effective knowledge and control of our environment, we can ensure the survival of our species for ages to come.

Our physical environment is ultimately the entire universe. We cannot, of course, know all there is to know about the universe now or ever. Instead, we can understand more and more beginning at a defined point: the self. By using the self as a reference point, we can master the universe bit by bit. We learn as we go, nibbling bits of information and digesting them as we are able.

Each aspect of our environment is defined by its relationship with all that exists. We cannot completely separate any aspect, including our selves, from the vital context of the whole. Because we can't define the whole universe, we concentrate on aspects of it that are the closest or most meaningful to us, or at least the most obvious. At best, we gain an incomplete understanding of each aspect. What seems to us remote or unimportant, we often ignore.

We don't necessarily recognize ourselves making these judgements, but we do so continuously. The result is that we each develop a personal system of priorities that we modify somewhat each moment of our lives. Something is either relevant to our immediate goals or it is not. We choose every action and make every decision according to our personal priorities. Our effectiveness is determined by how clearly we define our goals and how concentrated our efforts are in achieving them.

This book is intended to help us refocus our assessment of our physical environment to some slight degree. We all recognize the macroscopic elements of our immediate environment: we see the sky and the grass of the natural world, and the concrete and glass of the man-made world. What we don't recognize are the elements of nature we contact through the soul. Although we can survive nicely in the short term (as many of us are currently doing) with no appreciation whatsoever of the soul, a knowledge of the soul and the worlds it interacts with can aid us greatly in improving our lives—and in coming to terms with corporeal death.

The soul's existence has been recognized by every known human society. Although many people do not view the soul as a scientific concept (and therefore not real), most people still believe the soul exists in one form or another. The problem that faces us is in defining its physical properties in spite of its intangible nature. This problem can be resolved to some degree by not demanding to view the soul in sensory terms only; for the most part, the soul is a decidedly extrasensory entity.

The soul is not something you have so much as it is something you are. It is the life force, an energy structure that defines your personal nature. It is a part of the physical universe, having form and cohesion in its own terms. While it uses corporeal organisms for its survival and evolution, it separates from the organism at death. The discarnate phase occurs under the precise physical circumstances of the Afterlife, a world that is physically closer to you now than you probably realize. Eventually the discarnate soul joins another organism. This is the cycle of reincarnation.

Most cultural beliefs regarding the soul include some recognition of reincarnation. Modern Christianity, the predominant religion in the Western world, is something of an exception, though even Christianity makes mention of the reincarnation of certain prophets (the belief that John the Baptist was the reincarnated Elijah, for instance). Reincarnation is the means by which the soul interacts with its environment in order to sustain itself. As we shall see, the discarnate soul's perception of its environment is quite different from the perceptions of the corporeal senses.

Because the soul is not readily perceived by the naked eye or by the sense of touch does not mean it can't exist or that it has no physical properties. There are many things that exist without tangible evidence. For example, the physical nature of thought eludes us but we can't seriously argue that thought does not exist. The soul is rather like the intrinsic stuff of atoms, existing on a plane of reality that is so far removed from our macroscopic perceptions that we have trouble dealing with it in terms of its physical nature. However, my guides have dictated to me a brief outline of the soul's physical structure, which I shall repeat here. (A much fuller description is found in my first book, *Man's Unending Quest*.)

The soul consists of two fundamental classes of energy. One, soul-energy, is the basic substance of life—a stable base for the ongoing existence of the soul. The other, life-energy, is a secondary energy form generated by the living processes of the biological (or corporeal) body. The life-energy that survives the incarnation is converted to soul-energy following the death of the corporeal organism. This process provides for the retention of the experiences of that incarnation in the form of soul memories and for the growth and evolution of the soul.

During in-flesh life, the soul pervades the atomical structure of the corporeal body, adapting to the form of the body for the duration of the incarnation. When the body dies, the soul separates and the flesh begins to decompose. There is no evidence whatsoever to suggest that the soul dies with the body. On the contrary, what little evidence exists supports the idea that the soul leaves the body in a sustained and organized form. Further, human cultures have universally arrived at very similar beliefs of the life force, that it does survive death and, usually, that it can reincarnate. To me, these beliefs indicate that something inherent in the human being presses us to believe in the soul's survival. That inherent something, I believe, is the soul itself.

Unfortunately, little can be done to make the soul more tangible to our senses. Although energy-based, the soul is not detectable by any current technology. Furthermore, there is little scientific interest in researching the physical nature of the soul. This does not surprise me given the historical pressures on science to yield tangible evidence of all it studies. What *does* surprise me is the lack of interest on the part of our religious institutions to understand what the soul is and how it interacts with divine agents. Presumably, if we believe in divine forces, be it a single God or a multiplicity of gods, we must also believe they have some form or substance. Both science and religion seem content to accept the view that incorporeal nature is undiscoverable nature. However, I am not.

I no longer accept the casual attitude many people in industrialized societies have recently adopted. This is the attitude that if you die and find yourself still conscious, fine and good; if not, then it doesn't matter anyway. My contact with my guides has convinced me beyond any doubt that the soul does survive bodily death. I am also convinced that the soul has genuine physical form, even though this form is essentially incorporeal. The essence of the theory I am putting forward in this book is that the soul consists of an organization of matter that is nonatomical, yet still physical and very much a part of nature. I have adequate empirical evidence to support this belief. Among others, these experiences have included foreknowledge of future events, telepathic communication over great distances, and contact with intelligences of noncorporeal nature. I know that what I have experienced are just tastes of what can be achieved by a human soul unrestrained by the organic body.

My experiences are too real for me to ignore. Although I can't share them broadly except through the written word, sufficient numbers of people experience the same and similar events that I am quite comfortable with my new view of the universe. Furthermore, I know that my guides have opened my mind to truths I would not otherwise have accepted. I believe my life is richer for it.

I am not the first person to write about such experiences. Psychic phenomena have faded in and out of the literary marketplace for centuries. Many other writers have published books describing contacts with their guides. The body of such literature is large and growing larger, beginning with man's first written works and continuing to the present day. Throughout history the message has been the same: we are not alone. Man has been a guided species since his origin. I can easily see why the guides are usually called gods, because to us they *are* gods. They have stimulated our lives and religions, guiding us to ever higher goals. They encourage us to take on tasks we would not otherwise assume; they reach out to us even when our corporeal senses distract us from the vision of the soul. My personal guides have encouraged me to write this book; your guides, perhaps unknown to you, encourage you in all you do.

The role of this book is to bridge divergent worlds. It recognizes the two faces of man, the material self and the spiritual self. It seeks to draw those two selves into one through a greater understanding of the soul, its environment, and the many wonderful lifeforms that populate its environment. It does so within the context of modern science, laying out an expanded paradigm that can serve future research. It touches on familiar subjects in new ways and introduces new subjects in a familiar and, I hope, enjoyable context. The need for such books should be obvious: we cannot take full control of our lives until we understand our soul's nature as well as we understand our biological nature. This understanding, we should fully realize, is a product of a multidimensional physical nature that includes many parallel—and fascinating—worlds. Although such understanding can and will take centuries to form, each day will bring progress. Every day we will do as we have always done: learn more of ourselves and our place in an infinite universe.

Chapter One
A NEW PARADIGM

The universe is infinite. It is not infinite in all directions, as we understand the notion of physical space, but it is indeed infinite in terms of duration and physical existence. This infinity is much broader, deeper, and extensive than three-dimensional space allows.

Three-dimensional space is a physical subset of the universe. It is our primary environment, a context for our daily experience that we rarely challenge. We feel secure in our perceptions of it, and we resist efforts to disprove popular ideas that result from these perceptions. If our eyes tell us that the sun travels across the sky, we only slowly relinquish that idea to more accurate theories of celestial movements.

In the following pages, I'll illustrate how time and events have led us to misinterpret our place in the universe. I will contend that our focus on three-dimensional space and time has caused us to ignore crucial aspects of our existence. These aspects also affect our daily experience and relate to the physical nature of the soul.

The soul is not a popular concept in the modern world because it is associated with aging philosophies and ideas. However, the concept bears rejuvenation. With that goal in mind, I hope to provide a reasonable paradigm of the soul's environment. This paradigm involves considerable restructuring of many popular ideas, including how most of us view the physical universe.

I must add that I do not use the word soul in a religious sense, but in the interests of accuracy. Some readers may be averse to the term, but I believe it has great value. The word, unlike any other, conveys certain unconditional meanings. One is that the soul is the whole life force, whereas such terms as psyche, mind, or ego describe only aspects of the life force. A second is that the soul survives bodily death. Finally, the traditional understanding is that the soul is associated with nonterrestrial entities (gods, spirits, angels, and many other entities) that influence its earthly endeavors for better or worse. I emphatically wish to retain all three of these connotations; their inherent truth may not be obvious but each is in principle valid. This book will show how each is reasonable in the context of an open universe.

Again, I stress that I am not writing a religious work. Although many of my ideas deal with matters of religious concern, my views will remain consistently secular. I am interested in the principles that

10

govern the deepest aspects of human life. Naturally, this means some ground is shared with man's religions. But my ideas draw more on secular knowledge, general philosophy, and the disciplines of science. There is an undeniable spirituality to the human race. Our secular institutions have failed to come to terms with this spirituality. Rather than ignore it, I believe we should understand it, and grow through that understanding. There is much to be learned from man's spiritual nature. I don't think we should turn from a concept such as the soul just because it isn't fashionable. To turn away from the soul is in essence to say there is no soul—a position unsupported by any proved facts. My work has grown out of a willingness to think about ancient ideas in new terms. In so doing, I believe I have made some very valuable discoveries about the nature of the human being and the universe.

Although I use many methods common to science, I cannot present this book as a scientific work. This is because I have also indulged in practices not generally accepted by science. Even so, such techniques are valid means of acquiring knowledge. One such technique is automatic writing, a form of mediumistic communciations. Automatic writing, or soul-writing as it is more properly called, involves two (or more) parties. One is the human agent, such as myself. The second is an external agent. This external agent may or may not be from a nonterrestrial plane, as communications between incarnate individuals can occur at the soul level with or without the conscious knowledge of the waking mind.

For the most part, the information I am using in this book is derived from nonhuman agents from other physical planes. In broad terms, we can call these agents nonterrestrial intelligences—nonterrestrial because even they refer to our plane as "terrestrial earth". They refer to the planet as a whole as Earth. (The capitalized "E" denotes the whole planet, including all its parallel planes, of which terrestrial earth is but one. Souls, at least in my experience, have a defined etymology that is used for language-based communications, one element of which is to capitalize certain terms to denote a specific usage of a word that can otherwise be freely used in its uncapitalized form. Often the capitalized term denotes a whole or total concept. Therefore "Earth" is the total planet, all planes included, whereas "earth" can be used much as we do in everyday English to mean the terrestrial world we inhabit. Also, I use the term "nonterrestrial", rather than "extraterrestrial", so the term won't be confused with visitors from outer space. The nonterrestrials I am talking about might be described as visitors from *inner* space.)

I have tested much of the information herein to the best of my abilities; I have endeavored to present it in light of modern understandings of physical nature. However, the subject matter deliberately steps beyond currently accepted physical theory; I cannot, therefore, present it as proved fact. Still, I am convinced that both the information and its unseen sources are highly reliable. I must rely on my readers to share in some way my point of view (even if only temporarily while reading this book), that is, the view that man is not the only highly intelligent form of life in this universe, nor within the framework of this planet.

Other intelligent life can communicate with individual human beings through extrasensory means. This communication occurs via physical channels of consciousness established between the communicants as a form of telepathy. This type of telepathy is so common that we usually don't recognize it for what it is. Some of the events that we view as insight, intuition, or inspiration are really thoughts projected into our minds by external entities. This is not to say that we never have original thoughts, but rather we are not *always* as original as we are inclined to believe.

Occasionally, channeled communications are controlled. In my case, I am quite aware of both controlled and spontaneous communications. By controlled I mean communications that are initiated and directed with the full conscious awareness of the waking mind. In essence, I am a student whose teachers do not share this corporeal existence, but who are interested in this world. They channel information through me because of natural relationships between my consciousness and theirs. These natural relationships are quite complex. To understand them requires an understanding of the multidimensional nature of the universe, which this book in some small way begins to explore.

My teachers, or guides as I call them, intend firstly to educate me. In a loosely defined way, I am their charge, a sort of younger, less experienced brother to be educated. Although there are potentially billions of such guides (as each human being has his own guides), only a few are directly involved in my writing. These form a personal hierarchy of consciousness that is directed at specific goals, one of which is writing this book. They guide me as part of their purpose, and I write as part of mine.

As a writer, I am communicating through my books what I have learned from my guides and my own experiences. Occasionally people ask me why they don't have similar experiences. More often, though, they are quick to mention their own experiences of the paranormal.

There are many reasons why the so-called paranormal is not always taken seriously. For one thing, people fear ridicule. They understand their milieu and recognize when something won't be readily accepted. They may then hesitate to report it, or may even disregard it in their own minds, preferring not to disturb their image of reality. If the event involves nonterrestrial life or anything they identify as spiritual in nature, they may recall their religious unbringing and assume they have contacted their god or some holy or spiritual representative.

For the most part, modern society has decided not to accept the existence of nonterrestrial life until it is demonstrated in scientific terms. This means that although our lives are still influenced by nonterrestrial intelligences, the influence has to a great degree gone "underground", or more specifically, has been excluded from surface-level awareness. Of course I am talking here in generalities, because many people (including myself) have surface-level awareness of non-terrestrial contacts. On the whole, however, people do not readily tune themselves into nonterrestrial worlds. Often, their nonterrestrial contacts occur only in dreams or in subtle manipulations of their thoughts. If you are not attuned to such occurrences, you probably won't recognize them for what they are.

Some people insist that it is impossible for life to exist outside the corporeal body; they are not apt, either, to believe that noncorporeal lifeforms exist all around them in other physical planes. But we should remember that in spite of all man's knowledge no one knows what life is or how it works. We do not see what life is; we only see the manifestation of it in plants and animals. And we see how that life can so obviously pass from the corporeal organism. We don't see what happens to it then, where it goes, or where it came from in the first place. The nature of life is the greatest mystery of our time.

Life does survive the corporeal body. All human societies have developed beliefs in the survival of the soul. These beliefs stem from more than wishful thinking: they represent a natural tendency stemming from a natural fact. I cannot prove this statement, nor can I expect anyone to accept it at face value. I do, however, expect it to be given fair consideration. If the life force does not survive, why do most people believe that it does? The laws of statistics indicate that in a 50/50 situation—belief in survival of the soul versus no such belief—there should be a 50/50 incidence of belief for either side. Historically, such is not the case. Something is weighting the odds vastly in favor of belief in the soul. I believe that something is the soul itself.

Likewise, I cannot prove the existence of lifeforms in worlds parallel to ours—for that matter, I can't even prove my *own* existence. I can only be convinced of my existence because I am able to question it. Likewise, I am convinced by the weight of my own experiences that I have communicated with noncorporeal lifeforms. These experiences have often been extraordinary, combining elements of various forms of extrasensory perception (ESP). Through automatic writing and other mediumistic techniques, I have been informed of events in the future which came to pass exactly as foreseen. I have also been informed of historical facts about which I had no prior knowledge; these were subsequently verified by library research. My guides have even given me personal advice that has been enormously beneficial when I followed it. When I ignored it or wasn't sufficiently adventurous to act on it, I usually had cause for regret.

Many of my experiences have been out of the ordinary, but not unique. There are many paranormal experiences that regularly occur. ESP experiences are probably the most common. People have for centuries successfully predicted the future (precognition); perceived objects or events at great distance without mechanical aid (clairvoyance); and experienced nonsensory forms of communication (telepathy). I have experienced all of these many times and in many different ways. But however stimulating and revealing, these experiences are not the subject of this book; they merely led me to write it.

Mediumship, like ESP phenomena, continues to be a part of the human experience in spite of science's disfavor. I am convinced mediumship is just a form of telepathy. Other ESP experiences are often associated with mediumship, although they do not appear to be required for mediumship to occur. This leads me to believe there are laws of consciousness binding these events together. I view them not so much as paranormal events as normal events science has not yet fully documented. Even so, there is much documentation. The ESP phenomena have been tested in controlled laboratory settings for more than a century and the data are quite conclusive.

Furthermore, there are many documented case histories of paranormal events of all kinds that line the bookstore shelves. Though science has failed to be greatly stirred by these events, no one either has been able to lay them to rest. Just as proof is difficult to compile, so is disproof. Again, I judge the tenacity of the phenomena as part of the human experience to be circumstantial evidence in their favor. When dealing with real but intangible events of consciousness, proof is a hard master. But what proof do we ask of the greatest single nonsensory event of our everyday lives, common thought? To date, there is no conclusive evidence to show that thought is entirely a sensory product. Nor will there ever be.

When dealing with events of consciousness, the most convincing tool is direct experience. No one can convince someone who experiences vivid precognition that the experience is not real. Likewise, I fully accept the possibility of communicating with entities from other planes because I have experienced such communications. However, when I speak of such an event to other people, it is not necessarily an experience they can share. I am judged only, as I should be, on the basis of my rational arguments, and what tangible evidence I can offer.

Still, I maintain my assumption that the soul can shed the corporeal body and survive independently. I state this as fact, even though I do not have proof. Without getting into the arguments for and against faith, I only state it as fact because I am aware of a physical consciousness which has given me experiences that do not require the corporeal body. That body, I have come to accept, is only a tool used for learning. It is the mechanism by which I interact with this world. But I only interact with this world according to the efforts of my consciousness. That consciousness in its full-blown glory I call the soul.

It is unfortunate that I cannot share my experiences widely with people of this world except through the written word. I must somehow translate nonsensory events into a sensory event, the reading of this book; I regret that much is lost in the translation. However, my experiences are real. They are imposing evidence from my own perspective for what I have learned from my guides. I continually discover new information in books, journals, human contacts, and a myriad of other sources that supports what my guides have taught me. But more than any reason or logic or proof, I *feel* that their information is correct. I believe that this material broadens man's current knowledge. I also believe that it is valuable as a theory of consciousness and a theory of the physical universe. Given that no human knowledge I am aware of disproves it, it should stand as a theory to be tested. Then only time will determine in man's empirical eyes how accurate the theory is.

The concept of channeled information is not new, having existed since at least the time of Moses. What isn't clear is the source. Rather than blindly accept that the source is God (or Jehova, or Allah, or some other divine agency), I feel it is necessary to discern the actual nature of the source. But in spite of the vast array of information my guides have given me, to date they have not been very open about their own nature. I can say little more than that they are entities of a higher order than man.

These entitites take an interest in our development because of a natural relationship between us. They are in part responsible for the development of human civilization. They can communicate with us on many levels, and one level is a form of inter-plane telepathy. This is the channeling I speak of. It is also a variation of the religious theme of prayer; often, when prayers are said and answers apparently given, communication has occurred with entities such as our guides. Broadly speaking, each one of us is guided by such entities. Some of us may prefer to call them gods (and with acceptable reason), but I prefer to call them guides. Godhood, in the sense taught me by my guides, is a term reserved for even higher aspects of life and consciousness.

The theory of mediumship is not generally popular in the Western world, even (if not especially) with those who regularly pray. It seems to me that when mankind has had such historical devotion to higher beings we would make greater efforts to discover their nature. Instead, Western societies have developed an implicit model of the universe that doesn't readily accept the existence of nonterrestrial life. Many people believe terrestrial earth holds all the life that exists, and three-dimensional space holds the entire universe. Although time may do more to change such ideas than I will, I hope my ideas will appeal to readers who enjoy having their conceptions challenged, as mine were when I first encountered my guides.

My entry into the mystical world of mediumship was a sudden one. I had had psychic experiences before, but it wasn't until I was introduced to techniques such as automatic writing that I truly broke through to other planes. Suddenly these communications were real, inescapable, and very valid. There was a definite interaction between my senses and the nonsensory consciousness of other entities. It was a view of the paranormal I hadn't really had to face before. There were some very shaky moments in which I doubted my own sanity, as often happens with psychic experiences of such an extraordinary nature. However, I eventually became quite comfortable with the mechanisms of mediumship, and the new ideas mediumship engendered. It was for me a very momentous break with my preconceptions.

Mediumship to me is now just another tool of communication. I find it no more amazing than ordinary conversation between two people in the same room. The key point to remember is that *life* communicates with *life*. The mechanisms used can vary dramatically. Communicating with another plane is just a variation of the basic processes which allow thoughts to drive speech. The mechanics of speech are known to a degree but the mechanics of thought are not. And speech does not exist without the thinking entity. Likewise, telepathy is a physical human experience, and one which I hope will seem less esoteric after you read this book.

To enter into a conversation with a noncorporeal entity requires only the will of both parties and a telepathic channel. You can communicate telepathically or mediumistically with discarnate souls who have known life among the legions of earth, with entities that have little relationship to humans at all, or even with other incarnate humans. The nature of the communication can be sophisticated and intellectualized or primal and instinctual. It all depends on the levels of consciousness used, the skills of the individuals involved, and the environmental conditions prevalent at the time. It happens all the time; it is so common on a primal level that we scarcely note it in our everyday lives.

As I came to learn more of human nature, I realized that mental contact with my guides is not a new thing. I had just never recognized it as such before. I found that my new "recognized" relationship is merely an extension of a much more basic relationship. This basic relationship is available to all of us. All of us, whether or not we consciously recognize it, have our own personal guides. Contact is not always established on a mental plane, but there is a precise order to our individual guidance nonetheless. The contact is more often than not at the subliminal level. External influences on our ideas and courses of action therefore surface as impulse. In many ways, given our current attitudes toward external intelligences, the subliminal influence makes the task of guidance easier. Acceptable results are achieved.

The explicit contact that I have achieved with my guides is necessary to attain my goals. Most people, having chosen different goals, do not require such contact in their daily lives. However, this does not mean they cannot achieve it under appropriate circumstances. There are many levels at which contact can be established, not all of them obvious to the waking mind. The waking mind forms the most familiar part of the in-flesh personality. The primary personality (let's use the term "ego") is only one element of the soul.

Concurrent with the ego is a set of personalities that belongs to the base soul. These personalities are the personalities of former incarnations that live on in a fixed form of soul memory. In other words, the base soul is a base of consciousness which helps form a new personality each time the soul joins a new body. This new personality is then the primary guide for an incarnation in flesh.

At any given time, however, secondary personalities can be synthesized by the base consciousness. This very natural phenomenon run amok is the disorder of multiple personalities. Normally, however, it works to form the basis for communications with other entities external to the self. The nature of each personality enables it to contact certain other personalities external to the self. The interactions thus established can then be engineered into daily life.

Contact with other entities can be established in other ways. It occurs through dreams, intuition, and direct planting of thoughts in the mind by other levels of consciousness and by other entities. I regularly experience all these forms of contact, more intensely at some times than others. It is usually quite obvious when a contact has been made: the thought processes differ from my own, new information is transmitted, and there are often biological symptoms—a peculiar tingling of the scalp or skin of the back, for example. I have also experienced long-term changes in my body chemistry that are coincident with my experience as a medium.

These sensory experiences have reinforced the extrasensory communications in a dramatic way. Although anyone feeling a tingle is not necessarily communicating with another plane, it is indeed possible that nonterrestrial (or at least extrasensory) communication is occurring. Determining whether nonterrestrial communication has occurred is always to some extent subjective. The experience can be obvious or subtle, and there is no machine that can unmistakably identify the phenomenon. However, I do use my own base of sensory experiences to analyze extrasensory experiences as they happen. There is little doubt when a strong nonterrestrial communication has occurred.

I must stress that nothing is as convincing as direct experience. We base all our assessments of reality on experience; we only trust the third-party reports of scientists or journalists because we know they can be challenged. Even then, we often refuse to believe things we don't want to believe if it means refuting our own experiences or deeply held beliefs. Until the paranormal is effectively and objectively explored, the only convincing method of verifying such phenomena is individual experience. Thus, I acknowledge that I can't prove the ideas in this book; I can only set the stage for others to test these ideas directly. In time, I expect these ideas to become a part of our everyday understanding, accepted as readily as we accept the existence of atoms.

My confidence in the information I am presenting here arises from its consistency with known phenomena, including both normal phenomena (that is, accepted through scientific verification) and paranormal phenomena (that is, unexplained events reported in anecdotal terms). Over the years, my guides have given me information that consistently coheres to their overall theory and binds the known facts of science with the lesser known events of the paranormal. I must add here that it is *their* theory. Left to my own devices, I would never have come up with a theory of nature such as this. Until I experienced the radical intellectual and physiological changes wrought by contact with my guides, my ideas were stubbornly fixed along very common Western lines of thought. (We should note that each of us is the intellectual product of a culture, and we each accept implicitly the precepts of our native culture with little or no question.)

As the guides add new data, I am always impressed by its freshness. Unlike my own creative processes, the channeling *adds* to my knowledge instead of just using my existing knowledge in a creative way. This addition of knowledge is a critical factor in determining that the communication is with external entities, rather than a purely internal process. Interestingly enough, my abilities as a medium for the most part function at the discretion of my guides. Because I am not a natural psychic, I suspect that special efforts are required on both my part and the part of those who communicate with me to set up a relatively uninhibited channel. The key difference between my mediumship and that of a natural psychic is that unlike the psychic I don't lose consciousness during the communication. I am always totally aware of the words being communicated.

One point I would like to impress on anyone who is new to the idea of channeled information is that no communication is perfect. There is a great tendency among the uninitiated to expect or demand perfect answers to any question, especially questions regarding the future. Such demands are naive and unrealistic. Though mediumship often involves clairvoyant and precognitive elements as well as telepathy, these elements are not essential to the communication. Mediumship should not be used as a means of fortune telling, whether seriously or as a parlor game. Even so, I am not aware of any medium who does not have a wealth of clairvoyant and precognitive experiences to describe, many of them documented and corroborrated by witnesses.

Like any conversation, there is much potential for error in telepathic transmission. As well as errors in perception, there are physical limitations imposed by environmental influences. The communication is definitely "channeled", using a set portion of the mind's energy spectrum. (All living energy occurs within specific wave patterns or frequencies that are detectable in their own context—that is, by other living energies occupying a similar spectrum.) A telepathic communication is analogous to the telephone, which uses only sufficient bandwidth of the voice frequency spectrum to make voices reasonably intelligible and recognizable. In a telepathic communication, a message may be relatively uninhibited or scarcely possible. Yet, in all cases, there are limitations. Regrettably for us, most of these limitations are ours.

The human mind does not receive *any* communication in absolutely pure form. Communications based on language are especially imperfect because of the limitations of vocabulary. (Can you truly describe the color of a flower to a blind person who has never seen color or a flower?) In channeling information to me, for example, the guides have to work through my own limited vocabulary. They have to communicate to me concepts that require very extensive technical language, for which man has developed neither terminology nor technology. Although we have many technologies quite advanced in measuring electromagnetic, gravitational, and nuclear effects, we have no technologies whatsoever that can measure life-energy.

There are other limitations. I have attempted to write this book in a way that is not overly simplistic, and yet still clearly conveys the essence of complicated concepts. The information is based on what I have learned from my patient guides. At the same time, I have taken liberties in its presentation to better serve the needs of my readers. The concept of channeled information remains foreign to many people in our society, but it is not as esoteric as one might think. What we are missing is a coherent base of information that provides a framework or model within which such phenomena as nonterrestrial contacts can be studied and understood. It is my intent to provide at least part of that model.

Our current model of the physical universe is inadequate because we live in a shielded world. That shielding is as much the result of social and intellectual organizations as it is of any requisite of nature. In striving to strengthen ourselves in some ways, we have weakened ourselves in others. Where once the human race saw life in every stone, now it sees only atoms. This book, like many books born of contact with the unknown, is just one effort to help us look again into the mysteries of nature with open minds. Perhaps we can again see what our forefathers saw, but with greater understanding. And from that understanding can grow a new, more effective paradigm of nature.

Chapter Two
The Mystery of Life

I have always been interested in the nature of reality. To me, all of nature is a mystery waiting to be explored. Life, more than anything else, is a mystery of nature. We do not need to delve into the unknown reaches of the human psyche for mysteries, because nature is mysterious even in our common, everyday terms. Television, magazines, and books bring into our homes the exotic wonders of the natural world. The sky, forests, and seas are filled with creatures of unbelievable talents—frogs that carry fertilized eggs in their mouths until tiny, fully formed froglets issue forth; fish that walk on land; fragile monarch butterflies that fly unerringly to a single wintering ground thousands of miles away, weathering even hurricanes on the way. Evolution, in its age-old quest for a better way, has sculpted marvels that we wouldn't believe if we couldn't observe them, even if only through the lens of someone else's camera.

But the greatest marvel of all cannot be photographed. That marvel is life itself. Life is the expression of our being, a miracle that defies human description. We recognize it, accept it, but fail utterly to understand it. We only know that we live, and in living we can find joy, sadness, and wisdom. We know there are whole worlds of consciousness within our own selves we have yet to explore, but we have little understanding of the mechanisms by which they function. Even the nature of life itself remains undiscovered.

We adapt well to this lack of understanding. Sometimes we even convince ourselves that we know more than we do. This has more to do with our need for the assurance of self-awareness than our need for truth. In fact, our world-view, we must acknowledge, is fraught with limitations, most hinging on our limited sensory perceptions. Our world reflects to us images of itself that we are able to only partially assimilate. We are aware of some of the mechanics of that assimilation, as the receptors of the body tell us in their own individual ways about a portion of our world. Intuitively, each of us is comfortable in knowing that the world is much as it appears.

But is it? Philosophers have worried that question for centuries. Scientists trudge their way through mountains of facts in search of truth. Theologians and mystics teach their understandings of reality. But the true nature of life—what it is and how it came to be—has never been determined.

I have found both science and mysticism useful in this quest: science for its presentation of facts; mysticism for its unbounded leaps into arenas of discovery science has yet to enter. But neither science nor mysticism is the sole key to nature. Both offer an approach to knowing the same reality, each in its own way. Both provide a means of viewing nature through progressive discovery. And because nature is ultimately unified, what one discovers, the other can share. Though we don't always view it so, the quest of the mystic is as valid as that of the scientist. Whatever truth either discovers is part of a single whole. Both scientist and mystic can discover the same truths.

Like most people in the industrialized world, I find in science the assurance of facts. Facts are the foundation of knowledge, and I find it comforting that science can discover so many facts about my environment: why the sky is blue, why grass is green. The aura of confidence and assurance provided by such information is so great, in fact, that as a child I often felt that everything was known.

Time marches on for all of us. I quickly learned that there are very large gaps in scientific knowledge. What personalized this realization for me was that some of those gaps relate directly to my own experience. For instance, I occasionally have dreams that come true. I don't mean wish fulfillment; I mean genuine glimpses of the future, exactly as it eventually occurs. A short dream comes and goes, usually scarcely noticed until the scene unfolds again, only in real life. I see the same sights, feel the same emotions, and exchange the same words with the same people. Often, it is a place I have never been to before, including people I have never met. Some psychic ability within me jumps forward in time to the ideas, emotions, and sensory images I will some day experience. Although there is no scientifically identified principle I know of that can explain these events, I nonetheless experience them quite regularly. Until science provides a suitable explanation of the phenomenon, I can't accept our current paradigm as complete.

I now refer to these experiences as precognitive dreams, though I used to look backwards when the event happened in real life and call it déjà vu. Although the incidents seldom have any apparent significance, they are strikingly accurate in portraying events that haven't yet occurred. In once instance, a dream gave me a short preview of an experience I would later have in Europe, though I hadn't yet visited Europe at the time of the dream. The dream was not really very remarkable except for one peculiar thing: a dark-haired man was talking to me, pointing up a street, and saying something about the "second fire". I noted the dream only because I awoke, startled at the use of the word fire, especially used in such a peculiar context. I wondered why my dream personna felt no threat from a fire, or even perceived any evidence of one.

Then, some weeks later, I travelled to Europe and suddenly found myself in the exact situation of my dream. The dark-haired man pointing up the street was the proprietor of a restaurant, giving me directions to a nearby hotel. When he said "second fire", he meant the second stoplight, translating the French word *feu* directly into its English equivalent of fire, rather than stoplight. It was just a delightful mistranslation. Perhaps significantly, I often have such experiences during trips and vacations, when I am encountering totally new experiences. I don't have as many around home, although there are occasional incidences. Perhaps this is only because I often fail to note them when they involve routine incidents.

Although precognitive dreams may seem impossibilities to many readers, there are many others who will nod as they read this, knowing they too have had such dreams or other kinds of premonitions. I have met many people who have had similar experiences and I have read about many more. Although such testimony is not sufficient to convince the skeptic, the experience of precognition is too vivid to be a mistake. You only have to experience it once to be fully convinced. Once you know it to exist, no one can tell you that you didn't really experience it. It is real, and cries out for explanation. In this case, science has little help to offer us.

Precognition is only one class of experience not explained in scientific terms. Other people have other types of experiences, equally strange and equally undeniable. In any gathering of people, a substantial number present will be able to tell of an incident in their own lives that steps outside the accepted bounds of scientific knowledge. The range of experiences is amazing. For example, although I have never seen a true apparition, a farmer once told me of an apparition he saw as a young man. He was driving a team of horses down a dark country road when an old woman suddenly appeared before the team. As the horses reared up, he reached for the brake to avoid running her down. When he turned his eyes back from the brake to the road, she was gone. She appeared and disappeared in an instant, but was real enough to frighten the horses.

Almost every person alive has encountered the unknown in some dramatic way. Few of us escape the mysteries of life. Usually, we wonder about our experiences and marvel at those of others. But seldom do we come to any firm understanding of what has happened. I began as a youth to study such mysteries in a casual way, the study becoming increasingly serious as I learned more. I soon noticed common threads running through many of the mysteries I read about, as if there were a range of as yet unknown natural laws at work. However, I retained the usual Western attitudes and assumptions. Although willing to consider new facts, I was largely unwilling to change my fundamental belief system or my way of thinking. Then I first experienced true mediumship. Suddenly, my whole belief system was shaken up. Although I believed myself to be open-minded I had not until then been forced to truly open my mind.

Although in the Western world we like to think of ourselves as open-minded, few of us are. True, we allow science to discover new facts and slowly reshape our attitudes, but at the same time, we hold the reins in firm check. We do not allow science to change too fast or too radically from our accepted assumptions. Like that of any other society, the predominant Western view has its cherished preconceptions. These preconceptions are based on habit, social tradition, and cultural beliefs. We accept them so readily that we often experience cultural shock when we go to another land and find that people there think in radically different ways than we do.

These cherished preconceptions interfere dramatically with our search for truth. They control what we are inclined to believe and ignore. Though we like to think we are unbiased and objective because we use the scientific method to derive facts, we forget that we interpret such facts according to our cultural and individual biases. If it suits us, we ignore facts that don't fit our favored ideas or disrupt our comfortable patterns of thought. For Western man, who has little time for spiritual quests when material quests seem more lucrative, this means much of our spiritual nature is ignored.

But if we are honest, we can make some progress. What spurs us to honesty is curiosity. When direct experience contradicts accepted theory, we are faced with a fundamental decision. Do we throw out the theory or the contradictory data? My curiosity made it impossible for me to ignore genuine aspects of my experience; I was eventually forced to reorganize my way of thinking. It was painful in many ways but I believe I now have a more accurate understanding of the nature of physical reality. This understanding does not so much change my life as give me a broader perspective in which to live it. I find this valuable. Given man's efforts to explore nature, I feel safe in saying that most people will find a similarly broadened perspective equally useful.

Reincarnation is an example of an area in which I revised my Western-style thinking. At first, I felt reincarnation to be a very distasteful idea. In Western writings the concept is usually pooh-poohed. That undoubtedly guided my thinking. Everything from supermarket scandal sheets to serious scientific writings reinforce the Western notion that reincarnation is just another crackpot superstition. Though this intellectual prejudice is now slowly changing, it still exists. Westerners, who have a dominant religion that has discouraged belief in reincarnation, have carried this bias over into their supposedly unbiased scientific viewpoint.

Because of this cultural bias, I was altogether unaware of reincarnation until my early teens. Later, after having read about it as an esoteric belief, I was surprised to learn that it is a belief shared by perhaps two-thirds of the human race. When I was introduced to the concept as a reality through mediumistic communications—something in itself frowned upon in the staid journals of science—I was doubly shocked. My first reactions were very negative; I had an egocentric repulsion for having been "someone else". Not only did I fail to see the beauty of reincarnation, I failed to appreciate it as the crucial aspect of human evolution that it is.

In time I became comfortable with the idea of reincarnation. As I became comfortable with it, I began to realize the implications of reincarnation in the evolution of life. It provides the meaning in life that most Westerners now find missing; it means that all our careful learning in our three-score-and-ten years on terrestrial earth is not wasted. Our experiences survive and help build a stronger and wiser soul. Though in the modern Western perspective the universe seems hopelessly closed, the physical reality of reincarnation holds open to us a door we just don't see. Believing or not, we all reincarnate because physical nature compels us to; we just fail to observe the process for what it is during our three-score-and-ten.

Reincarnation opens up the universe to us. It gives us the time to study all that we want to know. Through cycles of birth and consolidation, the soul grows and blossoms. With that important understanding, I soon lost my distaste for having been someone else. I realized that my current personality is only the latest of a series of personalities, each of which was as personal in its own time as this one is now. I have also realized that even though this personality *seems* to be my total self, I only have to think about how each of my daily memories gets tucked away somewhere far from my surface consciousness, only to surface again by will or accident, to realize how little of my total self is active on *this plane* at any one time. I now have no trouble at all in accepting that there is far more to my total self than I can ever view with terrestrial eyes.

The cultural and personal biases that caused me to reject the idea of reincarnation were forms of conceit. They clouded my ability to perceive a genuine facet of human existence. Rejection of a new idea is often based on an unwillingness to admit the imperfection of our accustomed beliefs. We know in our heart of hearts that our beliefs contain many imperfections, but this is painful to admit. If an idea is distasteful to us, it usually gains its distastefulness because of its strangeness. To someone else, however, the belief may be as normal as our belief that man has walked on the moon, which even now some old-timers refuse to accept, insisting instead that the government is just perpetuating a massive hoax. In remote parts of the world, some tribal peoples find such an idea too monstrously unusual to believe.

We believe man has been to the moon because we trust the authority of those who have reported this to us. But what proof do we really have? If we didn't *want* to believe, we wouldn't. All the videotapes, the moon rocks, and the burned out rockets would not convince us, because we know all these things can be easily faked.

As it happens, we do want to believe man has been to the moon, and we accept the evidence. However, we are not so willing to believe in reincarnation. In one case, we accept the evidence readily, in the other we do not. Still, reincarnation is part of the open system of life. We come into this world in the soul-state (joining the fetus in the fifth month of gestation) and leave it in the soul-state. We normally fail to remember the discarnate state once we are born in flesh (though there are many recorded exceptions that provide convincing evidence). Once in flesh, we view the world from the state of mind we can call the waking state, or what souls call the upper conscious. The conditions set by adjusting to a new corporeal body force the upper conscious to take precedence over other levels of consciousness in setting priorities of action. This is necessary for the survival of the bodily organism. In the process, memories of the discarnate soul-state and other incarnations are submerged. Our terrestrial lives therefore seem cloistered and unadmitting of foreign worlds.

Having a natural focus on the biological world, we have developed cultures and tools that reinforce that focus. We are fascinated by our machines, which in turn focus exclusively on this world. Our view of the universe is based on our perceptions of the cosmos. Our sciences derive facts from the known environment and base further explorations on those facts. We therefore tend to disregard phenomena that don't align with facts already familiar to us. We are slow to accept anything new. This is a restrictive way to look at the world, but it comes naturally to us as part of our biological orientation.

Our dominant perceptions are those of an animal organism. Lifeforms in our world inhabit biological ecosystems that largely determine their existence. This corporeal body is an organic womb that accepts little beyond sensory inputs. Nonsensory inputs are usually ignored or are treated as if they had an organic cause. The farmer and his horses, when they perceived the apparition of the woman suddenly before them, all behaved as if the woman was of this world. Although that was their most natural reaction, her sudden disappearance illustrates how it was somewhat futile.

Our lives in the flesh are geared to making us more efficient and successful here. We tend, therefore, to depend on the tools and perceptions most useful to us here. We have other abilities that we set aside while in flesh because they are of most direct service to us when we are in the soul-state. This does not mean, however, that they are completely unavailable to us now. It only means that we normally fail to use them.

As we evolve into entities that no longer rely solely on biological responses to the events of life, and use instead a certain degree of rational decision-making, we exclude even more of our unobtrusive abilities. Intelligence, while it enables us to understand so much about what we perceive, encourages us to study first what is most obvious. Less obvious phenomena are studied later. Such is the case with the soul. Because the soul is not obvious to the senses, we have devoted little time to understanding it in any meaningful way. We have acknowledged its existence through religion and made some effort to understand it through mysticism. At no time have we truly attempted to understand it in scientific terms.

The soul is a physical entity. It has physical properties and it acts according to physical laws. These properties enable it to transcend three-dimensional space and live within a context comprising two or more worlds. Even so, the soul always acts within a physical system. We tend to view the visible cosmos as all that exists, though there are other physical planes, their nature unknown to us in our biological context. Many of these other worlds are certainly known to us in the base levels of the soul's awareness.

Discovering the physical nature of the soul would spark a new direction for material science. Science is currently focused almost exclusively on atomically related phenomena—the spacetime cosmos that we can perceive with our senses and machines. The phenomena of the soul which are obvious to us (thought, memory, telepathic communications) are so familiar that we often forget how little we know about them.

Science has yet to find how such things as thought can be totally the products of chemistry, electromagnetism, and other atomical constructs. The real discovery of what mind is, and what soul is, remains for the future. We only have the intriguing preliminary findings of neurological research, findings that map the functions of the brain and indicate ways in which the corporeal body can influence the mind, personality, and behavior, but tell us nothing about the life force itself.

Because the soul has not been proved to exist, many people believe it cannot exist. In contrast, other people accept the existence of the soul as a matter of faith and do not even feel the need to challenge that faith with empirical research. To me, neither of these attitudes is satisfactory. Through personal experiences of out-of-the-body travel, contacts with nonterrestrial intelligences, and past-life recall, I am assured that the soul does survive bodily death. To satisfy my Western mind, therefore, it is imperative that the associated questions of the nature of the soul's survival be resolved in objective terms.

These answers will only be forthcoming in satisfactory terms if scientifically researched. The first step in scientific research is to formulate a hypothesis, an end to which this book is dedicated. My hypothesis is that the soul exists much as depicted (in general terms) by the world's religions, myths, and mystic philosophies. These traditions have drawn on the core of the human psyche, and no matter how diverse in terms of cultural, historical or geographical background, all hold amazing similarities. Carl Jung believed such similarities originated in what he called the collective unconscious. In actual fact, that "unconscious" is the base soul, the basic consciousness of each individual human being. Because each of us has a similar structure of consciousness (just as we have a similar structure of organic body), there are common aspects of consciousness that result in what Jung termed archetypes. Although Jung dealt mostly with symbolism, these archetypes actually have physical manifestation in human nature.

The Jungian archetypes pervade human mythologies, religions, and folklore. These cultural beliefs and legends express much of what man believes about the soul. My intent is not to dwell on comparative mythology or comparative religion, as much work is already published in these areas. Instead, I want to synthesize a coherent model of the soul and its environment. My primary source is the same as that of the ancient mystics: the base awareness of the human soul and the Guides of Man. I won't despair if these sources are not accepted in scientific terms in the short run. Because they are real, and eminently valid, they will someday be discovered and analyzed in objective terms.

The soul is not tangible to the corporeal senses the way atomic mass is. It is real, but its reality hinges on laws and principles our sciences have little knowledge about—and no immediate inclination to study. This does not mean there is no evidence of its existence; on the contrary, there is much evidence. This evidence exists in our very awareness, in our thoughts, feelings, and emotions. It exists in more tangible ways through our mystic traditions and in our religions, mythologies, and folklore. Most of all, there is mounting evidence of the soul in parapsychological research, in studies of the life-after-death or "near-death" phenomenon, and scientific investigation of unusual psychic events. None of this evidence, however, presents a conclusive image of what the human life force is.

Yet the fact remains that man has searched for the root of his being since his earliest days. A major point of religion, a universal experience of man, is to gain some insight into the spiritual realities of his existence. Religion is the succor of the soul, as science has become the succor of the modern mind. Still, most people seek in religion solace more than facts and knowledge. To preserve religion as a source of solace, many myths and assumptions are also preserved without being subjected to the scientific scrutiny that would otherwise separate facts from fallacies. Many religious concepts become a sort of taboo, as most scientists prefer to deal with issues not tainted by religious sentiment. No scientist I know of is trying to determine whether God has a direct influence on our world, though many scientists profess to believe in God. A few try to establish whether the survival of the soul is a valid concept, or attempt to explore ESP, or chase after reported miracles. Yet such pursuits win credibility very slowly, and must fight an enormous cultural prejudice in the process. The consequence is that we have very little scientific knowledge about God, the soul, and other worlds.

The growth of knowledge will change that someday. As science is even now peeking under the edges of human consciousness, it will eventually strike to the depths of our natural soul. We will someday fully understand that this entity is not so tied to the fragile and short-lived corporeal body as so many of us now think. This knowledge will then lead to the discovery of other worlds and the lifeforms therein. But again, this development will not be soon.

Human religion indicates that most people want some form of guidance by external entities. To that end, they pray, consult mystics, and learn occult techniques. At the same time, few really care to know what physical nature their guides have. To understand our place in this universe, however, we really must begin to understand our relationship with other worlds. Nonterrestrial entities do interact with us, and that interaction has a bearing on the quality of life in this world in terms of both our individual and collective existence.

The soul is a part of an environment that extends past the confines of this world and is in contact with other souls at all times. This means that whatever our minds are thinking, other souls potentially have access to those thoughts. The same holds true in reverse: potentially, we have access to the thoughts of other souls. There are physical checks and balances which determine whether such access is granted, or even possible.

The soul does not need words to communicate. It can communicate directly with other souls by projecting pure meaning into the other soul's consciousness. This "soul-to-soul telepathy" is the soul's natural means of communication. The communication can be translated into words, if that is desired, but is not usually practiced between discarnate souls in the same way that incarnate people speak to one another. The difference is one of process. In speech as we know it, one person forms an idea and strives to translate it into words, often with grave difficulty. Words too often only partially convey concepts, or worse, don't convey them accurately at all. In soul-to-soul telepathy, the concept is conveyed holistically, that is, as pure meaning. The transfer is direct, and is translated into language by the receiver only if that is how the receiver chooses to process it. Otherwise, the message is received, assimilated, and understood as it is given, in one quick flash.

Even while in flesh, souls use soul-to-soul telepathy at the base level of consciousness. Discarnate souls and incarnates alike can communicate freely at this base level without the surface consciousness being the slightest bit aware of what is being communicated. At times, glimmers of such communications will filter through in the form of dreams, impressions, impulses, or sudden thoughts. If a discarnate soul wishes to contact the waking personality, it must accept the conditions of channeling the contact through the base levels of consciousness, with the inherent risk of the message being garbled in the process. To minimize this problem, souls use a precise lexicon, or etymology.

In the etymology of the soul, words are chosen for precision of meaning. Souls prefer one usage where there are synonyms, the preferred usage being called a "soul word". An example is to say to "gather", but not "accumulate", knowledge. Having strictly defined usages reduces errors of communication. Because it is so often a powerful experience, there are very real dangers in miscommunication between a soul and an in-flesh personality. I always shudder when I read in the newspaper of an account of someone who goes on a murderous rampage because he heard voices ordering him to kill or destroy. I suspect these cases sometimes involve garbled reception of otherwise legitimate communications. The mechanisms of consciousness break down through a mental illness with tragic results.

The etymology I am familiar with, of course, is based on English. Because I am English-speaking, nonterrestrials communicate with me in a manner designed to be translated by my consciousness into English, as opposed to French or Swahili. The entities who communicate with me as a reporter of their ideas convey their messages to me in a manner I can understand and manipulate as a writer. This means the ideas are only communicated as effectively as I am able to receive and understand them. It also necessarily limits the communication; the end result is colored by my own individual base of experiences.

The value of my treatment of this material is, first, that it is driven by my human understanding. Much published text from channeled sources is transcribed verbatim. While many of the truths offered are of the highest nature, they are often stated in such a way that it is difficult to apply them to our world, or they can be interpreted any way the reader chooses. By presenting my guides' input in my own terms, I present it in a way I believe is more pertinent to our human experience. Also, I can discuss my first-hand experiences and understanding of human mysticism (particularly in regards to nonterrestrial phenomena) in a manner consistent to serve a modern, Western-educated audience that is hungry to *know*. Most works based on mystic techniques serve more ritualistic purposes. This does not mean I ignore the value and purpose of ritual, but only that my work should better suit the needs and wants of the secular reader.

It is interesting to note that human mythology and religion have always acknowledged nonterrestrial worlds and lifeforms. The beliefs are nearly universal among human societies: the belief in the survival of the soul, its passage to other worlds, and the influence on it by gods and lesser entities that inhabit these other worlds. My experience has demonstrated to me that these ideas are essentially correct, and I believe societies develop these ideas because of the innate human tendency to recognize its own truth.

The intuitive nature of man points more or less accurately to facts. My feeling (and my experience) indicates that many beliefs in the seemingly intangible are based on discoverable phenomena. Science lags in discovering many of the principles of nonsensory phenomena because such principles are aggravatingly difficult to deal with in objective terms. It takes time to build the models, equipment, and tests required for objective analysis of even accepted phenomena. If the soul is not accepted as a physical entity, we should not be surprised that its perceptions and mechanics are not being explored. To achieve meaningful data regarding the soul's physical nature under these circumstances could take centuries.

Still, science is moving towards a recognition of traditional truths, whether scientists are in general agreement or not. There are some very interesting ideas in modern physical theory that indicate the existence of alternate dimensions, parallel universes, and other manifestations that are not obvious to our cloistered senses. I think these theories describe some of the worlds that interact with us via nonsensory levels of consciousness. These neighboring worlds harbor intelligent life; though scientists dare not commit themselves to the view, they are ever eager to speculate. In time, and in their terms, I believe they will demonstrate what human mysticism has taught all along: that the human soul can reach into other worlds as populous and magnificent as this one. When science accepts this, we'll be far on our way to solving the mystery of life.

Chapter Three
THE ESSENCE OF NATURE

Science has struggled for centuries to define the nature of the universe. The prevalent modern view describes a four-dimensional system, consisting of three dimensions of space and one of time. This view originated with Albert Einstein, whose turn-of-the-century theories of relativity and "spacetime" revolutionized the common perception of the universe.

Until Einstein, the universe was perceived as functioning like a well-oiled machine, a collection of parts that interact in clearly defined ways. This view dates back to at least the 17th Century when Isaac Newton captured the essence of many complex physical functions in a few exceptionally well-stated laws. Newton's theories of inertia, gravity, motion, and force set the stage for the evolution of physical science for 200 years. In fact, Newtonian physics still provides adequate explanations for many physical events at the macroscopic level. The appeal of Newtonian physics is in how well it meshes with the everyday human perception of how nature works.

In the early 1900s, Einstein challenged the Newtonian model. Einstein looked very deeply into such things as how gravity affects not just material bodies such as orbiting planets, but space itself. He saw space and time as a single continuum, and he believed that gravity actually bends space. As proof, he calculated a minute disturbance in Mercury's orbit that Newton's theory of gravity fails to predict. This and the growing scientific knowledge of subatomic physics revealed deficiencies in how Newton—and most laymen even today— view physical nature.

In Newtonian physics as in everyday life time and space are regarded as constants. The natural human perception is that time passes at a steady, stable rate, and is common to all of us everywhere. Likewise, we expect measurements of space to be constant. After all, every action we take is predicated on such assumptions. However, Einstein demonstrated mathematically that many such assumptions are not true. Time, he pointed out, passes more quickly or slowly depending on the speed at which a material body travels. The faster you travel, the slower time passes. Time is also affected by gravity; the closer to a source of gravity, such as the earth or the sun, again the slower time passes. The differences in rates are slight—measured in billionths of seconds as they relate to any speed or gravity we experience—but are there nonetheless. And they have been demon-strated experimentally to be as Einstein predicted.

These experiments have typically involved highly precise atomic clocks which can detect minute differences in the rate at which subatomic matter oscillates. If an airplane is sent aloft equipped with an atomic clock while an identical clock, carefully synchronized, is left on the ground, the clocks will register different times depending on how long they are apart and their differences in altitude, speed, and direction (that is, whether travelling with or against the earth's spin). Einstein had to patiently await the invention of such clocks before his ideas were proved, but he was not surprised by the results. Ultimately, he crystallized a new perception of the universe, as Newton did before him.

By this time technology had begun its snowball advance into the 20th Century. With the aid of ever-more sophisticated equipment, physicists found that even the master wasn't perfect. Certain subtle discrepancies between experimental data and Einstein's predictions showed that relativity theory also had weak spots. Even as the world began to realize the implications of relativity, theoretical physics was pushing into a new frontier. The new physics was to cause Einstein much grief.

Einstein, unlike Newton, was still alive to bear the brunt of the assault on his ideas. Although his basic ideas were sound, he was eventually forced to yield on certain important issues to new data and new theories. Some of the new theories departed as radically from his view of nature as his departed from Newton's.

Although Einstein had shown how many of our fundamental assumptions about the universe are misperceptions, he still believed in its inherent order. As the years passed, he found himself in the center of a rising debate. The new physics was growing out of the study of subatomic particles, particles which were at times refusing to behave in the orderly way Einstein thought they should. As other physicists sought to account for the anomalies, Einstein refused to accept the new physics. "God does not play dice", he thundered. "Stop telling God what to do", was the reply. In the end, Einstein failed to stop the rise of quantum theory.

The new physics once again attacks the established world view of the universe. When Einstein published his theories of relativity, subatomic physics was in its infancy. It was the 1930s before the third of the primary subatomic particles (protons, electrons, and neutrons) had been identified. Since then, a plethora of particles have been identified. These particles have an amazing range of properties, the most striking being their seeming lack of substance. This very substantial cosmos, including all its stars and galaxies, is based on an incredible mish-mash of particles that have no apparent solidity whatsoever. They exist, they have properties, but no lowest common denominator of matter has yet been identified by science. Protons and neutrons are now seen to be composites of smaller particles called quarks. Electrons and certain other particles such as neutrinos are believed to be indivisible in their natural state. This knowledge has been derived from theory and experimentation. Experimentation typically uses particle accelerators, devices which can be miles in diameter, to smash atoms to bits. The resultant debris is still being cataloged, but remarkable patterns have already emerged. Physicists are now finding that there is order and organization within the atom, though not in terms fully consistent with macroscopic events. However, the order is there. It presents itself in the form of natural symmetries, such as in the balance between positively and negatively charged particles (nature strives to cancel out electric charge) and the matching of an anti-particle with most—if not all—known particles. For example, a negatively charged electron not only attempts to cancel the equivalent positive charge in a proton, but also has associated with it an "anti-electron", or positron. These symmetries and other discoveries are now leading physical theory in directions Einstein was unwilling to accept.

Physics is perhaps at an equivalent stage now in terms of classifying subatomic particles as zoologists were a century ago in classifying animal life. There are still major unresolved areas, such as the true nature of energy. Is energy best described as a wave, or as a particle? A photon, or unit of electromagnetic energy, has properties one would expect of both waves and particles. For the moment at least, physicists appear to be in consensus that photons are both wave and particle, or wave-particle. This may be accurate, because subatomic particles seem to be just as formless. The lowest common denominator of matter thus far detected are the quarks, a family of tiny, apparently formless particles with such whimsical type names as "charmed", "up", "down", and "strange". If one overall picture is emerging through the modern physics, it is that the entire cosmos in all its intricate construction has no identifiable solidity—at its root, matter appears as more of a suggestion of form than form itself.

Much of what subatomic physics has to teach us flies in the face of common sense. It reveals a level of activity that seems hopelessly detached from our macroscopic view of nature; what is valid in terms of cause and effect at our level is not necessarily valid for subatomics.

For example, we expect a certain action such as dropping a stone to have a predictable result: the stone falls. Not only so, but we know the exact rate of the fall.

In the subatomic world, such predictability is not always possible. Part of the problem is in determining the effects of an action. Because subatomic particles travel so fast—near the speed of light—and many have life-spans of such short duration, it is very difficult to track them. You can look at, say, an electron at one point but not trace its path. The path, unlike the trajectory of a bullet, seems to fan out into a range of potential paths, much like the wave pattern established by dropping a stone into water. Yet when pinpointed, the electron appears to have the characteristics of a particle. The uncertainties of prediction in the subatomic world are factored into equations using the famous Heisenberg uncertainty principle. Such mathematical techniques help us to understand nature through abstract models. In fact, the mathematical models of quantum theory are more descriptive of reality than any verbal description can ever be.

Mathematics is the language of physics. As far as we are concerned, it is also the language of physical nature. Everything that exists can be reduced to mathematical formula. The trick, of course, is to discover the right equations. Newton and Einstein were superbly gifted in this way. The elegance of their equations is in their simple statement of extraordinary truths; such equations reveal the essence of nature.

Regrettably, quantum physics requires a level of mathematical expertise beyond the average person. In a way, the new physics has become an esoteric art, available only to the initiated. However, enough of the theoretical models can be translated into layman's terms so that everyone can have some appreciation for the quantum universe. At some point, quantum theory must be fully integrated with our broader understanding of the cosmos. The macroscopic cosmos, though it has many superficial similarities to the world of particle physics, is actually a higher level of organization, responding to the deterministic laws of cause and effect in a much different way than the subatomic world. Because it is macroscopic—you might even say "mega-scopic"—the cosmos presents another view of nature.

To view the cosmos as a whole is almost as difficult as to envision the subatomic world. Even so, the cosmos has been mapped with incredible accuracy both in terms of space and time. Science has calculated both the diameter of the cosmos and its age. These measurements are possible because of the understanding of physical nature Einstein's theories gave us.

Einstein demonstrated that space itself can be warped or curved by gravity. This idea led to the notion of a finite cosmos and, later, to what has been called the expanding universe theory. The idea is that the cosmos erupted into being some 15 or 20 billion years ago in what has been dubbed the Big Bang. The Big Bang theory contends that the cosmos as we know it emerged from an infinitesimally small point called a singularity. Through some unknown cause, the cosmos emerged from nothing and commenced a lightning fast expansion that continues to this day. Although analysis of primal energies left over from the Big Bang enables scientists to determine the rate of expansion, it is not known whether new matter is still being created. However, it is generally accepted that space is actually stretching to accommodate the expansion; the galaxies are growing farther apart.

It is not known what the cosmos is expanding into, if anything, or what it emerged from. It is easy to say that it is expanding into "nothing" and emerged from "nothing", but this is hardly an answer at all. It does not describe the originating spark or clearly define what the edge of the cosmos may actually look like. At any rate, Einsteinian physics assures us that the edge of the cosmos is nothing at all like the walls of a goldfish bowl. In fact, some theories suggest that space may curve or twist back in on itself in such a way that a spaceship travelling straight away from earth may someday end up back here. The fact that space can be bent or warped by gravity lends credence to such ideas. Regardless, space is now accepted to have outer limits.

Within those boundaries, the quantity of matter is assumed to be finite at any given time, whether more is being created or not. This means, theoretically at least, that all atoms, photons, and other identifiable particles in the cosmos can be counted. Having a quantifiable amount of matter also supports the idea that the cosmos is finite. Science therefore tends to view the cosmos as a closed system. Unfortunately, when scientists speak of the cosmos as a closed system, they often use the term "universe". In the modern world, the terms "universe" and "cosmos" have become virtually synonomous. This is regrettable. The cosmos, in fact, is neither a closed system nor the entire universe. Though finite, the cosmos is linked to other systems.

In this book (and as defined in my dictionary), the term cosmos means the large-scale material organization of space. Space, coupled with time, defines the parameters of the cosmos. As far as many people are concerned, this is an adequate definition of the term universe as well. Even so, the dictionary defines "universe" as "all that exists everywhere". This includes all the cosmos with all its galaxies, its space, and its time. The key distinction is that it also includes anything that is beyond the cosmos. In other words, the term "cosmos" may include everything that science has defined; the term "universe" includes all that and everything else as well. What that everything else may be is the subject of the rest of this book.

Although the cosmos is a finite system, it is not the *only* system within the universe. On the contrary, even scientists speculate that there may be external systems. Rather than just accept four dimensions of spacetime as being everything that exists, some physicists have suggested that the universe comprises 11, 26, or even more dimensions. I am going to go further and suggest that there are infinite dimensions. This suggestion is based on two concepts: one is that the universe as a whole is infinite; the second is that there are infinite ways of *viewing* the universe.

This second point is important. We are living entities embued with a set of perceptions that force us to view our environment in a certain way. There is no reason to presuppose that our perceptions are wrong per se, but it is paramount that we recognize that our perceptions are *restricted*. For example, our perceptions of time as a straight-line progression of past to future is disputable at best if we accept the notion of precognition. The current scientific paradigm does not accept precognition as a valid event and therefore ignores the phenomenon altogether. As I discussed earlier, I cannot ignore it because for me it is a real and indisputable part of my living experience. I must therefore assume there is something about time that I—and the rest of humanity—do not understand.

Einstein's theories changed the scientific view of time. A burned-out star, for instance, collapses inwards on itself. If it is a particularly large star, it can achieve a density so great that all matter within it compresses to a minute point. The star becomes a black hole. The gravity at the surface of this black hole is so great it slows time virtually to a halt. If some imaginary observer were to descend to that level of physical density and later emerge, he might find that all eternity had passed in the macroscopic cosmos. Unfortunately for our imaginary observer, nothing in our cosmos appears to be powerful enough to escape the gravity field of a black hole. Such a feat would require an infinite amount of energy.

A similar concept is that an observer propelled to the speed of light could also witness the stopping of time. Time would slow as he accelerated closer and closer to the speed of light. If the observer consisted of atomical matter, his mass would also increase relative to his speed. Here, too, an infinite amount of energy would be required to propel atomic mass to the speed of light. But if we put aside the impracticalities of propelling atoms to the speed of light, and concentrate instead on propelling energies to that speed, the relativity of time becomes very close to our grasp. Considering that the soul is an energy form, we have to be aware of its potential to travel faster than the speed of light or to otherwise transcend that barrier.

In fact, the barrier imposed by the speed of light is one related to atomical matter. Atomical matter cannot go any faster, but the soul is not atomical. Life-energy is not forced to perceive through eyes that rely on light energy; a conscious entity can perceive directly at the speed of thought. How fast is that? I don't know, but I do know that a thought pattern can cross thousands of miles virtually instantaneously. If it travels outside the framework of time itself, perhaps it is more appropriate to speak of it in terms altogether unrelated to time, that is, not that time travels so many miles per second, but that thoughts are transferred in their own unique, non-time-consuming way.

Even while in flesh, portions of the soul can transcend the atomical system. Accepting that life-energies in general can outstrip the speed of light, what are the practical effects of this? Because time is linked to velocity, how does a soul—or other conscious unit—view time when travelling faster than the speed of light or outside time? Can it see the past and future as well as the present?

In fact, the soul does exactly that, viewing past, present, and future as symmetrical events. In planning its actions and "reading" the events of the future, it interlaces its projection of its own circumstances and desires with the circumstances and desires of other souls. It is in the interlacing of desires among many souls that instability, change, and evolution enter the picture. Free will, though largely limited because of existing physical conditions, always applies to some degree. This means that even if the soul can predict what is going to happen, there is some outside chance that some action of free will can alter the future.

Aspects of our consciousness can be aware of the future even in our own system. Through precognition, the mind can skip forward to events that have not yet occurred. The mind does this by tapping into the base conscious, where events have already been worked out by the base soul. There are various mechanisms for accessing these "memories" of the future, and I am personally familiar with several. The most startling are the dreams in which I see picture-perfect images out of my own future. In these cases, the precognition functions similarly to ordinary memories of the past; the mind reads data stored in the base level of consciousness and projects it into the surface consciousness.

Such precognition is not what we would consider usual or "normal" experience. Normally, the mind attempts to block out memories of the future because of the way such memories interfere with the decision-making processes of terrestrial life. When I have a precognitive dream, it is apparently the result of some minor slippage in an otherwise controlled process. An alternative explanation is that the dream is the result of a lower level of consciousness—or some other conscious entity, such as my guides—forcing an override of the "normal" screening effect provided by a layer of consciousness souls call the middle conscious. The middle conscious has the practical function of separating the upper conscious, the mind, from the base conscious, or the base soul. The reason for this protective barrier? It keeps us sane. Can you imagine what it would be like to know every moment of your future? You would lose all ability and motivation to face that future. By suppressing this knowledge, you are able to function in terms demanded by terrestrial realities, including the linear perception of time evident here.

The bottom line is that our perception of time as progressing in a linear fashion from past to future requires review if we are to understand how our system interacts with other systems of nonlinear orientations. Time outside our system is not linear as we perceive it. Instead, it is holistic; from outside this system, it is apparent that all time occurs in a universal instant. When outside the corporeal framework, this fact is evident to the soul. It can also be evident to the upper conscious—that is, our usual waking conscious—if we choose to expand our awareness somewhat. Although this expansion is not essential to our healthy functioning within this environment, it would help us to understand our overall place in the universe. On the whole, however, it is safe to assume that although time cannot survive without the universe, the universe can survive quite easily without time.

Time, like space, is a subsystem of the cosmos. Time, coupled with space and its composite matter, forms the cosmos. The cosmos, in turn, is a subsystem of a much greater entity still. The universe has many such layers. My guides describe a universe in which multitudes of very large systems, many orders of magnitude greater than the cosmos, interact in an ever-mixing, ever-changing way. The universe is alive with great systems forming, borrowing from others, self-destructing, and undergoing internal transformations of all kinds. All these systems and their subsystems have limits which define them as finite entities. The model of universe my guides present, therefore, is that of an infinite entity composed of infinite numbers of finite parts.

The universe, according to my guides, is at its most elemental level an infinite field. This field, or area of effect, has no fixed limits. There is no beginning, no end, no edges, no middle, no inside, no outside. It simply *is*. Within that infinite field, there are infinite patterns of infinite style and persuasion. At the heart of it all is something the guides call the universal force. This force is the practical effect experienced within the field. It is the source of the patterns. If the universal field conveys the idea of a *realm* of effect, the universal force conveys the idea of *how* it acts. A third concept my guides apply is the idea of energy, or substance. Substance in cosmic terms includes atoms, photons, and other entities such as gravitons (what some scientists believe to be the active agent of gravity). Cosmic substances are just a subset of universal substance. Each physical manifestation of activity within the universe involves some form of energy or substance. This energy or substance, in effect, is the universal force configured into something meaningful, something that can interact with other things.

This model is a very simple one. The infinity of the universe cannot be measured, but aspects of the universe can be separated conceptually for study. Each part of the universe, however or whatever you define a part, is therefore inherently finite. It has limits and properties, and can consequently interact with other parts that have limits and properties. The complex patterns that we can observe within our system, the cosmos, are irrefutable evidence that the universe is capable of organizing itself in complex ways. My guides suggest that it does this based on a single lowest common denominator they choose to call the universal force.

You may ask how this single universal force can construct all the complex entities in the cosmos and whatever else exists in an infinite universe. Consider string as an analogy. A single piece of string can be tied into many varieties of knots, knitted into sweaters, woven into intricate patterns, and treated in any number of ways. Like this simple piece of string, the universal force organizes and reorganizes itself constantly. Everything that exists is a complex arrangement of this single common denominator, arranged through a complex series of events that has culminated in this unique point that is now.

The universe can be viewed two ways: as a whole, and as a collection of parts. As a whole it is infinite. At the same time it is a collection of parts, each of which is finite in some way. To speak of a given property of the universe is to select one aspect of the whole and draw certain parameters around it. The very nature of drawing parameters around something means attaching to it inherent limits. In fact, this is precisely what we do when we speak of the cosmos, or atomics, or any other aspect of existence.

Parts can act with apparent independence. The amount or quality of independence depends on the nature of the part. Human beings act with more apparent unity of self than, say, the earth's oceans, which are really a single body of water surrounding all landmasses. Still, oceans and humans are equally integrated into the fabric of the universe. The apparent functional independence of the human being or an ocean is at once valid and a sham, depending as it does on selected—and therefore arbitrary—characteristics. Still, the concept of functional unity is a useful one, one that we require in order to organize our perceptions. It enables us to make sense of our environment and to interact with it in selective ways.

The interaction between any two aspects of nature depends on their respective properties and what forces act to combine them or keep them apart. Some interactions may not be apparent from certain points of view. For example, we know that smashing atoms produces, among other things, tiny particles called neutrinos. Neutrinos have very little interaction with matter as we know it. Yet they exist, and though difficult to trace and identify, they have been observed with the high technology now available.

Each aspect of nature has its own properties and attributes. The properties of the cosmos, for example, include space, time, matter, and so on. These properties are unlikely to be present in any other system, as other systems have their own unique properties. Yet all systems have as their ultimate source the essential substance of the universal field. This means that all properties interact, though there may be many, many intermediate steps linking any two properties chosen at random. With the arrival of science, man has become interested in tracing interactions in a very specific way. This analysis requires equipment that can sense the properties involved. As in finding a way to trace a neutrino's path, tracing the interactions between dissimilar systems can be next to impossible.

The essential properties of any system are unique within itself. There can be similarities between systems, but the essential factor that keeps systems separate—which gives them their definition as systems—is that they *do* have a unique set of properties. When properties are shared, interactions are obvious and easy to detect. Thus, shared properties tend to be part of a single system, or at least to be viewed that way by whomever or whatever cares to analyze the properties. When properties are sufficiently dissimilar so that they do not interact readily, they are usually considered to be part of different systems. Thus, space, time, and atomical matter are probably unique to the cosmos. These properties, in fact, *define* the cosmos. If there were other systems with these properties, we would be more directly aware of their existence.

Our mechanical devices—and our corporeal bodies—receive energy signals from compatible devices and material organizations. A radio receiver, for instance, receives radio waves; the human eye perceives light. If some other system outside the cosmos had the properties of radio waves or light, our radios or eyes would receive them as a natural course. We perceive the properties we are attuned to; properties we are not attuned to escape our attention. The conclusion we can draw from this is that major systems each have their own properties. In fact, the uniqueness of their respective properties are what causes them to behave as independent (but not closed) systems.

We can therefore define a physical system as a set of properties which causes it to act as a coherent entity. The component parts of one system may be a part of more than one system, or the system may appear to be discrete. The definition of the system depends to a large extent on what properties are selected for observation. We consider the cosmos to be defined by the properties of space, time, atomical matter, light, and so on. The combined effect of these properties is a system that we can define with a reasonable degree of authority. To the best of modern knowledge, the cosmos appears to be finite. What we cannot say is that the universe itself is finite.

If indeed the universe is infinite, a lot of unanswered questions suddenly become resolvable. An infinite universe does not require a beginning or end, so the question as to how the universe started or how it will end are moot. Likewise, too, are questions concerning the physical limits of the universe. However, these questions can be posed in regard to any and all *aspects* of the universe, as they all are relevant to parts of the whole. All the parts are finite, therefore all can be defined in finite terms. Their interactions can then be explored as part of an open system, a system which allows finite parts to interact in any variety of ways. This system can be called the open universe.

Chapter Four
THE OPEN UNIVERSE

Science today favors the idea of a closed universe. This bias is based on the fact that the best available information indicates the cosmos—or space and everything within space—is finite, and that there are outer limits or boundaries to space. To that end, science has developed a history of the cosmos. This view is somewhat myopic, however. It focuses on the universe as a system of spacetime, as opposed to an open system in which spacetime is just one subsystem.

In the open universe, innumerable systems have evolved, each with an identity derived from its internal principles and properties. Just as a human being is a distinct entity within a larger environment, large-scale universal systems act within specialized contexts. They interact while maintaining an essential identity of self. That identity, of course, is a manifestation of the properties that give them form.

It is difficult to accept concepts of infinity. Human beings have an ingrained desire to know the beginning and end of things. This motivates us to explore our environment and attempt to map its nature, origins, and destiny. To date, our exploration has led to an impressive model of the cosmos. This model represents our understanding of what we are and where we are located in space and time. If we were not curious to know when and how the universe began, we would not have discovered the age of the cosmos. But knowing the age of the cosmos does not mean we know the age of the universe.

Some scientists believe the expanding cosmos will someday reach a zenith and then collapse as dramatically as it was born. This collapse, believed to be some 20 billion years away, has been dubbed the Big Crunch. Scientists debate whether the Big Crunch is the end of everything or whether something else—perhaps another Big Bang— subsequently occurs. If the Big Crunch is followed by another Big Bang, then eventually another Big Crunch will occur. And then the cycle begins again. This is known as the oscillating universe theory— perhaps more accurately described as the oscillating *cosmos* theory.

This theory potentially provides for an infinite duration of time, if one views the Big Crunch as only suspending time until the next Big Bang. However, some troublesome questions remain. Whether we elect to believe that there was a single Big Bang or a multiplicity of them, we still don't know the *cause* of the first Big Bang. If there is more than one Big Crunch, what happens after the last one, if indeed there is a last one? And even if we establish that the universe is infinite in terms of time, what other qualities also possess infinity?

The oscillating cosmos theory describes a system that is closed at least in terms of space. It can only get so big before it collapses. Is it reasonable to assume that an entity that exists totally within one set of conditions—that enclosed by the conditions of space—is able to spontaneously generate and destroy matter? Or are agents external to the cosmos acting to create the conditions we know as the cosmos from some *other* set of conditions, that is, does something *else* create matter and the cosmos? If so, then the cosmos is not a *closed* system, but a *finite* one that interacts with other systems.

At the moment, the scientific consensus seems to be that the Big Bang occurred spontaneously. So far, scientists haven't mapped cosmic history quite to its very beginnings, although they do generally understand what has happened since the barest fraction of a second following the Big Bang. But no evidence exists as to what caused the Big Bang, or what went before, if not another cosmic incarnation. The cosmos, to the best of modern knowledge, appears to have popped into existence quite literally from nothing. Some scientists beg the question of universal origin altogether and point the curious to the disciplines of philosophy and theology for further discussion.

The origin of everything is indeed a great metaphysical question. Interestingly, human cultures have universally concluded that something as wonderful as the universe is no accident. They ascribe the process of Creation to a conscious power. Although this power has been assigned many names, the idea of a Creator is universal. This Creator may be seen as one or more entities, but even in multi-god systems of belief, a paramount god is usually viewed as the Creator. This idea neatly provides an answer to the question of what created the universe, but begs the question of who or what created the Creator.

Creation is too big a question to be answered here. However, I think it is fair to at least adopt a strategy for dealing with it. My strategy is to include the Creator, whoever or whatever it may prove to be, as part of the physical universe. The Creator is therefore included in the physical paradigm that I am expressing here. As I noted earlier, it is not necessary to understand all aspects of the universe to hold the notion of "all that exists". If a Creator exists, then as far as I am concerned, the Creator is part of the universe. In fact, there *is* a Creator, and this Creator is very much alive in every aspect of the universe. In effect, this Creator *is* the universe. What this means is that the universe created itself; this does not mean necessarily that it caused itself to emerge from nothing, but that it creates its current state out of its previous state. The universe is in a perpetual state of creation.

At this point, neither science nor metaphysics has the definitive answer for how the universe came to be. If we can identify a first event, we must ask what went before. Likewise, there can be no final event. The linear view of time demands that there always be a preceding event and a subsequent event to any point in time. This in itself leads to an understanding that the universe must be infinite in duration; if you can mentally step outside the bounds of time, you will have further evidence of the infinity of the universe. The universe is infinite. We can therefore never trace its origins, nor its end. We can only map its existence to points farther and farther from a fixed reference point. That reference point is our own existence in space and time.

We can never know all the aspects of the infinite universe because there is always more to discover. No matter how thoroughly we map, say, the origin and destiny of the cosmos, we have scarcely begun to map the nature of the universe. We study the universe from an expanding base of knowledge, but we still must use our own existence as a reference point. Whatever we discover is necessarily determined by what is *possible* for us to discover given our orientation and capabilities. We discovered the make-up of the cosmos first because that is where we are and what is most tangible to us. When we are ready, we will expand our quest to other aspects of the universe that are currently hidden from us.

If a spaceship were able to reach the edge of space, for example, it would not find any end of being, but a transformation. What exists as space would undergo a change so that it became something else; one system would end and another begin. The transformation would occur according to precise laws and for reasons demanded by physical nature. At the transition point, the predominant properties of one system undergo transformation according to the laws and properties of the new system. What defines the respective systems are the conditions of their interaction—how clearly or cleanly they shift from the properties of one to those of the other. To reach the edge of space, perhaps it would be necessary to travel faster than the speed of light. Such a speed would transform the atomical matter of our spacecraft and bodies into something quite different. If we survived the experience, we would undoubtedly encounter a system beyond our known cosmos. Its difference would not be that it is "someplace else" so much as "someplace different". The characteristics of the new existence would be fundamentally different than our current system.

Under the new rules, space and time might not even exist. As it happens, because the soul is not atomical it can make just such a journey.

The cosmos interacts with neighboring systems. The borders or boundaries are not distinct but delineate a change in state, where properties of a given elemental reality change radically. By analogy, consider the change of state when water freezes or boils into steam. The lessening or increase of heat energy in water can have a dramatic effect on its properties. The water moves from liquid to solid or gas. This happens without any intrinsic change in the water molecules themselves; only the rate of vibration speeds or slows.

Given different forces, say electrolysis, the water molecules can actually be broken apart into hydrogen and oxygen. Different forces still—fission or fusion, the splitting and fusing of atoms, respectively—can create different atomic elements: hydrogen atoms, which are the simplest atoms, can be fused to create more complex atoms; oxygen can be either fused into more complex atoms or broken apart into simpler atoms. Similarly, the properties of space can be altered given certain conditions (such as the presence of gravity.)

The various large-scale components or systems of the universe interact in very much the same way as small components such as water, hydrogen, and oxygen. There are laws governing all transformations. What constitutes a system is largely a matter of perception and definition. We view the cosmos as a system because we perceive it to have a coherent unity. From our point of view it makes sense to talk about systems being a part of or external to the cosmos. At the same time, we must keep in mind that the cosmos as a system is only really a part of an infinite universe, one which in its total self is an integrated whole.

There are two reasons why we are not aware of how our system interacts with sister systems. One is that we are naturally oblivious to much of our environment. Like a radio receiver that picks up only certain frequencies, we fail to perceive what we are not equipped to perceive. Second, we are not in the habit of paying attention to such interactions. Energy transformation between our system and others occurs all the time. However, we do not need to be aware of such activity any more than we need to be aware of our own internal processes such as the digestion of food proteins and their reconfiguration into human proteins. We only require that such transformation happens.

Energy is exchanged with other systems in many ways. We have technology that detects aspects of such exchanges, but scientists have yet to fully grasp the implications of the data. The most highly developed mechanism we have at our disposal for detecting such exchanges is the human body. Our corporeal organism has evolved as just such a device. It takes energy from this system (mostly from food) and reorganizes it so that it can be transported as part of the living consciousness to other planes. It, in essence, is a machine for transforming food energy to life-energy, which in turn is transformed to soul-energy. The transformation from food energy to life-energy occurs within the corporeal body; the transformation from life-energy to soul-energy occurs in the Afterlife.

The removal of energy from the cosmos to the Afterlife is critical to our existence. Our lives depend on the open transfer of energies across the boundaries between this system and the Afterlife—a neighboring system, though a neighbor in nonspatial terms. The transfer across the boundary is one described by many people who have died and been revived, and by astral travellers. They often describe it as a barrier of light, a crossing over. This description is very accurate. It is a natural impulse to describe this as "crossing over", and even to experience or perceive it in familiar terms such as crossing a river, going through a tunnel, or whatever. But the description of light is most accurate because it conveys a sense of an energy barrier between two systems. That is exactly what the boundary between our spatial system and our Afterlife, a nonspatial system, is. The transfer between systems is possible because of energy transformation. Like the biological process of osmosis, whereby certain chemical substances pass through cell walls while others are blocked, certain energies are blocked. Life-energy is such an energy.

Energy can be changed in many ways. It is the essential stuff or fuel of the universe. It has many forms. In our world alone, energy has a stunning variety of uses and manifestations. We use the kinetic energy of falling water, for example, to drive turbines. The turbines create electricity which in turn heats and lights buildings, carries telephone conversations, powers computers, and does so much more. Plants take sunlight—light energy—from the sun and use it to fuel the manufacture of proteins, carbohydrates, and other biological compounds. Animals, including man, eat plants to access this energy, reconfiguring the compounds according to their own processes and needs. Animals also feed on animals, creating quite complex food chains. The constant throughout the food chain is the transformation of energy and biochemicals from one state to another. Raw material is processed into something useful. The production of life-energy from food energy is just one aspect of this very complex chain of events.

The transformation of energy is something that is not perfectly understood. However, it has long been known that each transformation occurs according to perfect laws of conservation. When energy is transformed, nothing is lost. Whatever results from a transformation exactly equals what existed before. Though not all the kinetic energy of water can be transformed to electricity, the remainder is absorbed by the ground, transformed into heat, or carried on down the river as a lessened kinetic force. Whatever is present on the left-hand side of a physical equation must be fully accounted for by the right-hand side. Everything in the physical universe operates according to these demanding laws of conservation. Regardless of what changes occur within the universe, the whole is maintained.

Viewed as a whole, the universe is a single, uninterrupted field. It is the ultimate system. We divide it into subsystems, because our own existence makes it feasible to do so. In fact, our existence as discrete entities within the universe *demands* that we differentiate between subsystems. This differentiation, however, occurs within our perceptions of our environment. Though we can function as independent entities, we do so within an environment that is ultimately the entire universe. On a larger scale, the cosmos has its own form of independence. But it, too, depends on its context. No aspect of the universe is fully independent. Everything that exists interacts in some way, however remotely or indirectly, with everything else that exists.

The interaction of parts within the universe means that where one system such as the cosmos ends, another must begin. The ending point may be gradual or abrupt, but a transformation occurs between all systems. You could define your body, for example, as ending at the contact point with the air. If you move into water, the elements involved in the transition change, but the principle remains. Where your body ends, something else begins. It is the same with large-scale systems such as the cosmos. The edge of space and speed of light are two boundaries or limits; each of these is also the beginning of something else. The nature of the transition and what lies beyond remain to be determined. But the principle remains: where one system ends, another begins.

Each aspect of this universe is a portal to everything else that exists. There is nothing that is separated or removed from physical nature. If we discover how something is limited, we must then begin to explore the laws that govern that limitation—and the laws that govern its transformation into something else. The boundaries of the cosmos should not be viewed as the limits of the known universe, but as doorways to new horizons. Whether or not we acknowledge this, other worlds are critical to our existence. Why not open our minds to them and attempt to explore them however we can? In the short term, this may mean indulging in nonscientific practices such as mysticism. However, in time, the mystery of mysticism should give way to the understanding of science. Much of what we now view as mysticism will someday be accepted as well-understood principles of nature.

Science and mysticism must at some point integrate. Quantum physics is even now laying the groundwork for a truer view of the multidimensional universe. Rather than view mysticism as "supernatural", we should recognize it as a valid part of the human experience and use it for what it can teach us. Although much of mysticism seems incredible, keep in mind the incredible—but fully valid—achievements possible through the martial arts, yoga, and many other spiritual disciplines. And if that doesn't lift the corner of the veil for you, consider the evolution of science. The herbs and mystic rituals of primitives are still leading modern man to discoveries of new medicines and a greater understanding of human abilities of self-healing. There remains much untapped in the primitive religions of our race.

Many people view mysticism as being synonymous with "supernatural". I don't agree with this view. Mysticism, as I see it, is merely the manifestation of forces, powers, techniques, properties, and so on not yet classified in scientific terms. Although science has done a remarkable job in terms of predicting the discovery of new subatomic particles, black holes in space, and other physical phenomena, the usual sequence is for an event to be discovered first and explained later. There remains much about mysticism that is not yet explained. And, as mystic events are one by one explained, we will cease to view them as being mystical.

There is a particular realm of mysticism that science resists exploring. This is the realm of noncorporeal consciousness. Science would prefer to discover an atomical—that is, electro-chemical—basis for consciousness rather than have to expand its paradigm to include nonatomical planes. This is because our mainstream sciences—and the careers of our scientists—are focused on the forces of atomics. This is not surprising. Atoms fuel the activity of the galaxies. Our sun, for instance, is a huge fireball of nuclear activity. It is the source of energy for our planet and a gravitational anchor that keeps Earth from spinning off into space. And it is only a small star; there are billions upon billions of stars in the cosmos, all functioning on principles of atomics. With virtually everything that we perceive in our daily lives being the product of atoms, it is no wonder that we tend to think of physical nature preponderantly, if not exclusively, in atomical terms.

But atoms are only part of the universe; the atomical cosmos is only part of our environment. Our internal nature depends as much on the nonatomical as it does on this cosmos. The soul, though it uses this plane for its evolution, is not atomical in nature. Its constituent energies are part of the same family of energies as subatomic energies, but the specific energies are intrinsically different in configuration. If terrestrial earth suddenly became uninhabitable, the soul would still survive; it would be able to adapt to other planes. It is this ability to transcend atomics that has led to all the forms of human mysticism. What we perceive as being beyond our immediate world—beyond our atomical cosmos—we perceive as being within the realm of mysticism. This realm need not be considered "supernatural"; it need only be considered "nonatomical".

Mechanisms of consciousness transcend atomics. Consciousness does interact with the corporeal organism, primarily through the brain and nervous system, but is not exclusive to the biological organism. Much of our consciousness continues to interact with the souls of the Afterlife and entities from other planes even while we are in flesh. We are usually not aware of such communications in our waking conscious, but they occur nonetheless. Human consciousness functions similarly to a multiprocessor computer; each level of consciousness is like a separate processor, tracking its own tasks independently. In fact, when we build computers, we are actually attempting to reconstruct the architecture of our own consciousness, though there remain important differences between current machine intelligence and human intelligence.

The soul is our window to the open universe. Our corporeal receptors, our bodies, are conditioned to perceiving only the atomical plane, the cosmos. Likewise, our machines can only perceive atomical phenomena. An atomical device, be it the human body, a particle accelerator, an electron microscope, a radio telescope, or what have you, can only perceive material intrinsically compatible with itself. If a device such as the eye, a telescope or a microscope uses visible light to function, then it can only perceive things that reflect visible light. If it is to be detected at all, it must be by some other means; that is why there are radio-telescopes and electron microscopes. These devices allow things beyond the range of conventional light-based equipment to be examined. But even these more sophisticated tools have their limits; if any device is totally incompatible with a given phenomenon, then the phenomenon cannot be observed with that device. It's that simple.

Man's machines are intrinsically incompatible with the soul. The soul does exist and exists according to natural laws. However, these laws lie outside the province of atomics, so our atomical devices are of little or no use to us in analyzing the soul. We can measure brain waves as electrical patterns but we cannot measure and qualitatively analyze the substance of thought. Though we are thinking every waking moment, we have no acceptable scientific theories of what thought is.

To analyze the soul, we need to interact with it on its own terms. As long as we demand that all aspects of consciousness be explained in terms of atomic theory, we will fail to understand the nature of consciousness. There is little hope in the short term for any fundamental realization of this sort in scientific terms, but individually you can definitely do something to improve your personal understanding of the soul. This can be done by acknowledging the soul in its own terms and using its abilities to reveal its nature to you. In short, you must use your own mechanisms of consciousness to understand that consciousness.

Because of its nonatomical nature, nonatomical techniques are required to gain any immediate understanding of the soul. This means using mystic techniques. It also requires knowing something about what is possible. You must therefore study what is already known. There are thousands of books that offer great insight into the mechanics of consciousness. The spiritual works of all cultures are valuable, including the oral legends and folklore of primitive peoples. In fact, folklore is especially important because it reveals how unfettered human minds perceive their environment. From the modern vantage point, it may seem that primitives are unnecessarily superstitious with their concentration on spirits and other unseen life. From the soul's perspective, however, they are not so wrong

Armed with some background knowledge concerning human spirituality and myth, you may undertake some study of the sciences. It is important to measure your ideas against the exceptional data compiled through science. Usually it is not the data that are wrong so much as the human interpretations imposed on the data. That is why I can at once agree with the concept of a finite cosmos but extend the theory of an infinite universe. I disagree with the *interpretation* that because the cosmos is finite, it is therefore closed, and therefore the universe is finite. In fact, to the best of available scientific data, the cosmos is indeed an open system, just as I am contending in this book.

There is much truth in man's religions, his legends, and even his folklore. Science has made tremendous advances in explaining the behavior of the cosmos, both at the galactic level and at the subatomic level. However, science has failed to come to terms with human spirituality. That is why many scientists feel it necessary to go to church. Despite their knowledge of material nature, they appreciate their spiritual nature as much as the layman. It is one thing to state in a theory that the cosmos leaves no room for a soul or gods, but it is another to accept it totally. Unfortunately, this approach enforces a division of perspective; a single individual often holds one view of his material self while holding a seemingly incompatible view of his spiritual self. It is time, I think, that we began to consider our nature from a more holistic perspective.

In fact, the modern point of view inhibits our appreciation of our inherent spiritualism. Whereas it was relatively easy for primitive man to contact nonterrestrial guides, most people today are inhibited to even attempt this. There also a blocking effect derived from our focus on intellectual pursuits. The modern worker is more removed from the land than primitive man. To primitive man, the inherent spirituality of every rock and tree is obvious; he consequently constructs belief systems that reflect this reverence. In the modern world, we cloister our spirituality in small churches, churches which have less attendance every year. Our development suits our current purposes, but the cost is great. The resurgence of fundamentalism throughout the world indicates a sharp recoil against modern values. It represents an explosion of pent up need for a fulfillment of basic human spirituality.

Spirituality is a recognition of the internal self and its relationship with all other life. This includes life on other planes. Our mythologies do not necessarily portray such lifeforms perfectly, but do convey the essence of what they are. As my guides pointed out very early in our association, the spiritual entities that can contact the human world may not match our mythological and mystical definitions, but do fulfill many of the *roles* we ascribe to them. In some very simplistic way, the mythologies of man reflect the essence of a universal order and our place in it. At some innate level, our creative consciousness can tune into our entire evolution.

It is my experience that these abilities are available to the mind as well as the base soul. Like developing mind and body to the point at which one blow of the hand breaks through a half-dozen bricks, the mind and body can be attuned to reading its own awareness of itself. I believe such awareness was at work in our myth-makers. I believe a similar sensitivity enables us to communicate with entities from other planes. Human myth is geared to two ends: one is to explain what happens in the world; the other is to control it in some way. This second end has led to the formation of religious thought and practices.

Religion is the ritualization of beliefs within human society. We have many religions, all of which assume the existence of a higher world. This higher world involves the surviving essence, the soul, of the individual. It is a place where the soul goes when the body dies. It is also a place where other entities dwell, entities which do not join human flesh. These entities are often perceived to be concerned with our welfare, though harmful and indifferent entities are also described. Usually, a supreme force is acknowledged, whether a god leading gods (such as Zeus) or some form of overlaying universal consciousness. These gods and spiritual entities are appealed to in prayer, meditation, and ritual.

I think the development of religion and structured ritual reflects an inherent understanding of the natural universal order. I don't think we would create ideas of gods if there were no gods or some physical manifestation that stimulated belief in gods. Nor do I think we would create ideas of heaven, eternal life, or the survival of the soul if such things did not exist in some context. The trick, of course, is to find the right context. We should seek out that context in any way we can, scientifically or otherwise. In the short term, it seems as though science won't yield the answers we are seeking. However, the ancient techniques of mysticism can be easily modified for present-day use. If in the short term we want to learn about other worlds, I don't see any alternative but to step beyond the strictures of the scientific method.

As a mystic more than a scientist, I have only a small regret that I cannot prove my experiences using the scientific method. But unfortunately these experiences are intangible to existing technology. Nor do they fit any existing scientific paradigm. However, I am fully aware of what I have experienced, and that experience is indelible. I am also aware of the implications of what I have learned. At best, I can express some rudimentary ideas as to the mechanics of the soul, other worlds, and the entities therein. I must then leave the field open to debate and (I hope) to eventual systematic research.

But even with such limitations, I believe we can make worthwhile contributions to human knowledge through mysticism. What excites me most is that I am beginning to understand how the ancient forces of mysticism may be integrated into a scientific model. Some of these theories may lead to an understanding of the principles of parallel planes such as my guides describe. According to my guides, each plane is a set of dimensions governed by physical laws and forces. Our plane is governed by the laws and principles of spacetime, whereas the various planes on which my guides dwell are governed by different laws.

In time there may be some resolution of science and mysticism. In the meantime, human knowledge must converge on the same point from two separate directions: that there are other worlds within this planetary sphere that interact with ours through conscious entities such as my guides. Both science and mysticism show how this is possible. What we lack is the specific model of the universe that includes those worlds. My guides have endeavored to provide me with such a model, albeit in very general terms.

To truly understand the nature of the universe, we need to break out of our conventional patterns of thought. When we think of space, we think of a three-dimensional coordinate system of height, width, and depth. When we think of time, we visualize the present flowing irrepressably forward, leaving the past like flotsam behind a falling tide. We become comfortable with our way of thinking and rarely challenge the assumptions that evolve from it. Instead, we should twist our minds in unaccustomed directions. If we think in terms of three dimensions, we should try to visualize four or six. If we see time as flowing from past to present, we should think of a system in which there is no time, where all is now.

Such exercises may not tell us what lies beyond the edge of space or what it is like to live without time. Still, they help us maintain a flexibility of mind—a child-like innocence, perhaps—that is so often lacking in modern man. To even begin to appreciate the true nature of the universe, we must surrender our notions that the universe can be explained in terms of a limited number of dimensions, forces, or properties. We must think in terms of infinite dimensions comprising infinite coordinate systems. Only then will we have the vision and imagination to understand the open universe.

Chapter 5
A DOORWAY TO UNDERSTANDING

The soul is a doorway to understanding. It is the mechanism by which we learn; the fact that we learn is a measure of our status as a lifeform. Once learned, knowledge remains a part of the soul and is available to all aspects of its being throughout its existence. This means all the knowledge ever gathered by our souls is available to us at each moment of our lives. Mostly, this innate knowledge is used during our terrestrial lives as wisdom and instinct. Sometimes, however, we can dip directly into the knowledge of the soul if we learn the proper techniques. These techniques are many and diverse, but can be described in broad terms as the mystic arts.

The mystic arts have always led us in our quest into the nature of extended reality. These are the techniques science doesn't understand and sometimes scorns. Yet they are also the roots of science; scientists today either forget or ignore the mystical ideas of many of the founding fathers of science. But it was often the willingness of the scientist to dabble in mysticism that caused the birth of a new science. Psychiatry today is still on a course set by Sigmund Freud a century ago, a course set in a wild hodge-podge of ideas, many of which are laughable by today's standards. Carl Jung provided the next great push for that still-emerging science; many of his ideas were rooted in his studies of the soul, astrology, and other esoteric relationships between the human psyche and the environment. There is much still to be learned from our mystic past and our psychic roots. We have only to develop our hidden and often forgotten talents.

The mystic arts allow us to reach beyond our known selves and our known world. Essentially, our known selves are our egos, to use Jung's term. The ego is the surface personality, which has its roots in what Jung termed the unconscious. This unconscious is what I call the base conscious, or the base soul. It is the root of our being as living entities, and the greatest tool at our disposal for divining truth.

The base soul is the foundation on which the mind and the ego as a whole rest. The mind only part of the physical structure of consciousness, or the total psyche. The psyche is the physical structure of consciousness that supports intelligence, thought, feelings, desire, and all those characteristics we ascribe to life but so often view only in abstract terms. These characteristics are not shared by all lifeforms, but are indeed shared by all lifeforms that can be designated as soul-entities. The base soul is formed from the experiences of many past lives; the mind is formed from your current lifetime. As two elements of consciousness, the base soul and mind form the living awareness of the soul.

Souls are a particular type or class of lifeform, which is characterized by a specific and highly specialized unity of self. We view this unity as independence, seeing each human being (and therefore the soul of that human being) as an independent entity. There are many orders and races of soul-entities, the Human Race being only one of them. In fact, all animal consciousnesses are soul-entities, as are many entities on other planes and other worlds. The term "soul" applies to a specific architecture of consciousness. Other forms of life—plants, for example—have less individuality in their living architecture and are therefore not considered soul-entities. The classification of lifeforms is not the subject of this book, but it is interesting to note that life-energies tend to develop characteristics that suit the vehicles they use.

It is difficult to describe the differences and similarities between the life-energies of plants, humans, and other entities, such as the Guides of Man. This is because the nature of life and consciousness remains virtually unexplored in our world. Granted, Jungianism has sketched the outlines of human consciousness in some rudimentary way, and some experimental work has been done on humans and animals. But even the best of modern theories of consciousness are analogous, perhaps, to old maps that showed only the coastline of Africa. Calling the awareness of the base soul the "unconscious" is much the same as calling the interior of Africa the "Dark Continent". It is only dark and foreboding to those who know nothing about it. To the base consciousness itself, the "unconscious" is as illuminated as the interior of Africa has always been to its inhabitants.

Science is still on the outside looking in as far as the base conscious is concerned. The waking mind cannot peer into every aspect of the soul, but it can be more aware of the total self than it is currently. What is missing is an effective paradigm of consciousness that accepts the "unconscious" as a true awareness. Although we have the raw elements of this understanding at our fingertips, we have yet to pull it all together. Jung has so far come the closest. However, psychology today is entering into a greater and greater fascination with neurology, and therefore in many ways is growing away from the insights offered by Jung. Neurology shows us how the mind is affected by the body, and to some degree also the reverse. It does not show us how consciousness works, or even what it is. Jung, on the other hand, was aware of the soul as an entity. He is still revered for his work in human symbology, but science tends to forget he also mapped the outlines of a consciousness that is not yet being explored in any systematic way.

This consciousness is the soul. The mind, the only true awareness science accepts, is only part of the soul. The whole soul is a multi-level structure of consciousness. Each level is tightly coupled to each of the other levels. The base of this structure is a pool of multi-incarnational experience called the base soul. The mind, as part of the upper or waking conscious, is only partially aware of the base soul. However, the base soul is wholly aware of the mind, and directs most of the mind's activities either directly or indirectly. This means you are currently acting on the wills and desires of your base soul as much as those of your waking mind. Although the mind has its own motivations, these are developed within the period of a single incarnation. They grow out of the motivations of the base soul, formed within your biological and social context.

There is a great deal of interaction between the surface mind (your waking personality) and the base soul. This interaction forms a unity of consciousness that can't truly be dissected and cast into separate portions, but certain dividing lines are sufficiently clear as to provide a working model.

The base soul forms the core of your being. It is a foundation on which your familiar ego is based, and contains all the memories of your past lives. It is, in fact, the consolidation of all your past lives. Your current life-experiences are being gathered in a separate energy structure, called the Spirit, which is the product of the biological body. Your familiar ego is largely the manifestation of the Spirit, a life-energy body similar to the base soul, but a more volatile and temporal structure. The Spirit is constructed upon the soul's joining of the fetus in the fifth month of pregnancy and is sustained throughout the corporeal incarnation by the mechanics of the biological body.

Memories of your current life are stored in the life-energy of the Spirit, and are only integrated into the base soul following the death of the flesh. While in flesh, the base soul and Spirit function as separate systems, one supporting the base conscious and the other supporting a surface consciousness, or what souls call the upper conscious.

Your goals and objectives in life are stimulated by the goals and objectives of the base soul. These are brought to your life with the base soul and represent the most pressing needs of your development. It is somewhat difficult here to define what "you" are. You are a mixture of several primary elements, the base soul, Spirit, and corporeal body. All three combine to make you what you are. However, you probably identify most with your surface awareness, or the consciousness of the Spirit. This is the portion of yourself that supports your waking mind. It is the "I" of your thoughts. However, your base soul—which holds a much broader range of experiences—is equally "you". Perhaps the only part that is really not "you" is the biological body you inhabit: it is really just a chemical construct that you use to gather experience.

Trying to sort out your various levels of consciousness is very much like trying to sort out your goals. There are a few very obvious goals—such as survival, having a family, a career, or whatever—that you are very much aware of. At the same time, there are many other goals, some of which you meet and resolve as you go about your life (such as buying a new coat), and others that you work at steadily (such as being a generous person). Your goals are derived from two basic mechanisms: your base soul and your body. Both brings needs to your life. The body must be cared for and nourished to survive. You therefore expend a great deal of energy caring for it. At the same time, you have higher goals, which are brought to your life by your base soul. Your success in achieving them, however, is largely determined by the strengths and abilities of not just your base soul and body, but this third portion of yourself, the Spirit.

The Spirit is a discrete life-energy body that can actually leave the corporeal body for brief durations. This is called astral projection. This ability is not too significant in terms of gathering experience (at least as far as most of us are concerned), but it illustrates how independent it is of both the base soul and the corporeal body. The Spirit's conscious powers are largely centered in the mind, which is the only part of human consciousness about which science has any great deal to say. But the mind's conscious powers largely mirror those of the base soul. If, for instance, you want to be a violinist, surgeon or poet, and pursue such a career throughout your life, your desire originates in your base soul. But your success will be determined by how well your total self functions. It is not enough to have strong desires, you must also have talent, dedication, ambition, drive, and many other skills. Not least of these skills will be determined by the actual abilities of your own corporeal body.

Because of the enormous range of talents required to achieve even a few carefully selected goals, most of us tend to focus on a few basic interests throughout our lifetime. This does not mean we do not have broad interests, as many of us do. It does, however, mean that most of us can only be good at a few things, or a few *types* of things. These skills are the result of the peculiar combination of body, soul, and mind that composes each of us as a human being. Although the base soul retains many desires and wishes for future exploration, it cannot appease all of them at once, that is, in one lifetime. If all the desires of the soul were to explode into one lifetime, neither the biological organism nor the mind could handle them successfully.

Under normal circumstances, the desires and wishes of the base soul are carefully orchestrated in terms of their influence in a corporeal lifetime. This orchestration is conducted by a special layer of consciousness called the middle conscious. This layer is derived from the physical juxtaposition of the Spirit and base soul. The upper conscious (a product of the Spirit) and the base conscious (a product of the base soul) interact as virtually separate awarenesses, communicating with each other through the middle conscious. This middle layer filters the information that passes between the mind and base soul. In fact, most information is well screened. Few past-life memories are allowed to pass from base soul to mind. Similarly, contacts of the base soul by external agents are usually submerged and do not find their way into the upper conscious, except through dreams, notions, inspirations, and other mechanisms of consciousness.

The middle conscious is the reason why few of us are familiar with many, if any, past-life memories. The most common interaction with our pool of past-life experiences is during dreams. However, you can develop past-life recall techniques that can be used at will. These are means of making the often intuitive guidance of the base soul more objective, or at least obvious. As the primary guide to all human endeavor, the base soul is a very valuable source of information about ourselves and an aid in making crucial decisions—decisions that may well affect the rest of our lives.

The general structure of consciousness, therefore, consists of an upper, middle, and base conscious. These layers each interact in their own ways with each other and with the corporeal body. The corporeal body has an impact on each, some more than others. For example, the corporeal body is responsible for gathering and processing the chemical substances (food) that generate the energies used by the Spirit. The Spirit, in turn, is eventually incorporated into the base soul, but not until after the death of the flesh. While alive and well, however, the corporeal body is very much a part of the conscious unit. It imposes its own needs on the entity, and we all go to great lengths to satisfy those needs.

The needs of the corporeal body eventually find their way into the patterns of the base soul, though this takes several incarnations. The instincts you experience are the product of many generations of the habits of the corporeal animal surviving in the genetic pool. These instincts are then experienced by the soul during in-flesh life. After several incarnations, the life-patterns of a particular animal become part of the soul's own habits. The soul finds itself adopting the animal instincts as its own. In time, the instincts of one become the other's.

For example, whenever a soul incarnates in our world, the base soul submerges its own awareness beneath the corporeal folds. The fetus gradually develops an awareness independent of its mother's cellular structure, gathering its own will and nature about it. It develops a life-energy structure based on the joining of sperm and ovum; what was part of the father and mother now join and become a common and unique entity. This remains a primitive consciousness until such time as the embryo develops sufficiently for the soul to join it.

The soul, which is the product of many similar incarnations, joins not just the biological body, but also the neophyte awareness that is developing within this body. The joining severs a conscious alliance between the life-energy awareness of the fetus with that of the mother; at this stage, the fetus is a genuine individual. This does not mean there is no longer a close relationship with the mother; it only means that a new person and a distinct life-energy unit has developed. This is the portion of consciousness that, as it develops into a more organized structure of consciousness, becomes the Spirit of the new person. This Spirit absorbs from the body, the base soul, the mother, and even the external environment the key elements of its new personality. To a large extent, this personality is determined by the past-life experiences of the base soul and the biochemistry of the corporeal body.

The physical joining of soul and fetus occurs in the fifth month because the fetus is then sufficiently developed to survive independently of the mother. Granted, its chances of doing so if aborted are still very slim. However, until that point, the life-energy of the mother keeps the fetus alive. The fetus gets its food from its mother and is aided in processing its energy byproducts into life-energy by the mother's life-energy. This is a symbiotic relationship, as opposed to a parasitic one, and the joining of the soul to the fetus is a key factor in enabling the fetus to survive on its own. In fact, without the presence of the soul, the aborted fetus would eventually die much as a plant cutting withers and dies out of water and nourishment. And unlike plants, animals do not have the ability to root themselves if water and soil alone are present.

The physical joining actually stimulates the creation of the Spirit body, a secondary energy structure that carries its own motivations, wills, desires, emotions, and other characteristics of life much as we know them in our surface personality. In effect, this *is* our surface personality, the product of the sudden fusion of the base soul and corporeal body. The Spirit is formed by physical processes of base soul and corporeal body interacting. These interactions occur automatically upon the soul's joining the flesh, as automatically and nearly as vigorously as when pure sodium is placed in water. What happens is that certain reactive particles of energy both on the part of the soul and corporeal body recombine to form the secondary energy body. The life-energy of the Spirit is then sustained by the physical nourishment of the corporeal organism. When you eat, you not only sustain the proteins of your body, but also the life-energy of the Spirit. This life-energy tends to be unstable and breaks down rapidly. The result is body heat. The overall coherence of the Spirit is maintained through constant replenishment, just as the coherence and continuity of your cellular structure is maintained by the biochemicals you ingest.

Once created in the womb, the upper conscious—or the mind— begins incorporating impressions and images from its environment and, filtered through the middle conscious, from the base soul. Because of its dependence on the atomical environment, the atomical environment becomes its primary focus of concentration. As we grow up, we are only vaguely aware of the abilities and awareness of the base soul. The surface personality, not fully developed until age two, floats on a sea of awareness that remains deep, dark, and mysterious even to our most enlightened mystics and insightful psychologists. It is at the mercy of the tempests of the chemical soup of the corporeal organism, the shocks of sudden stimulations of dormant past-life memories, and the vagaries of its own awareness and tenuous existence.

But the mind, being new with each incarnation, also has the precious quality of innocence. It is a new consciousness, a new attempt at life, and an opportunity to correct or make up for past failings. Its consciousness is guided by the instinctual urges and emotions that arise from the soul's reincarnational history and from the direct physical influences of the flesh itself. In its very newness, it has the advantage of approaching the world with a fresh perspective. At the same time, however, it is also susceptible to the misconceptions of the society it joins, misconceptions that survive because the base soul never has full control of the organism while in flesh.

The mind, in other words, is educated by the incarnational world, its people, and its focus of consciousness, and not by the base conscious of the soul. The knowledge of the base soul is held apart from the mind for most of the waking life, its presence a guiding one as opposed to a source of facts and information. The mind is a blank slate filled by its experiences in the incarnational world. Though guided by the base soul, it is also very easily misguided by its incarnational experiences. Our societies pass on their teachings by word of mouth and through social institutions; consequently, biases, hatreds, misconceptions, and ignorance survive because each new mind absorbs these learnings as part of its physical environment, starting even before birth. It accepts them as naturally as it accepts physical sensations. The experience of the base soul, though acting as an engine providing drive, motivation and direction, is definitely sheltered. Its influence filters into the mind only in bits and pieces through dreams and ideas, which are always screened by the mind's own natural protective mechanisms. If a new idea is felt to be threatening (and it often is), it is not quickly accepted.

This situation appears at first to be a major disadvantage of in-flesh life. Perhaps it is, but it is also the factor that makes in-flesh life possible at all. The middle conscious shields the growing and strengthening mind from the total awareness of the base soul. Developmentally at the fetal stage and even later, this protection is required to enable the mind to establish physical control over the biological organism. But as in so many other human dichotomies, the positive need to control the corporeal body is somewhat offset by the fact that the knowledge of the soul is to a large extent lost to the mind. The base soul, then, has as its most effective means of aiding the mind only its muted voice: the two-edged voice of wisdom and conscience stems from the soul.

This division of consciousness is more to the disadvantage of the mind—a lesser awareness—than the base soul. We may well identify more with the consciousness of the mind, but our ignorance of the activities of our own base soul do not inhibit it at all. Even while the mind, or upper conscious, proceeds about its worldly concerns, the base soul is energetically conducting *its* affairs. It operates concurrently to the mind, though on a different plane of understanding. It is setting up experiences, communicating with other entities—on this plane and others—and analyzing its environment in stunning detail. The soul can explore nature in a way the mind can only vaguely appreciate. It can assimilate data in instants that mankind has spent thousands of years painstakingly gathering and archiving in libraries. Although we can train our minds to access this knowledge, and can even develop mental ESP abilities similar to those of the base soul, we rarely do. Instead, the human mind is increasingly directed towards the slow, methodical processes of intellectual reason. Not all human cultures have as totally given themselves over to this method as the industrialized nations, but the human trend is in this direction.

The linear pattern of rational thought is time-consuming, but one that we as a species have evolved to use, for better or worse. The price is that our less obvious mental talents, such as nonsensory perceptions, lay undeveloped and atrophying for lack of exercised use. To a greater and greater degree, the terrestrial experience of man is being intellectualized. We learn more and more by study and thought, rather than by holistic assimilation of experience as the base soul does.

As we further develop our dependence on our intellect, we blunt even the biological senses we depend on for our daily survival. Though we are "sense-oriented", we choose to pry ourselves further and further from our native instincts and abilities. For better or worse, we are becoming entities of linear reason, separated from our instinctual nature as souls and our biological nature as animals. I don't think it is necessary to lose either our nonsensory or sensory skills while we develop our intellectual skills. It is only necessary to exercise these skills to make them ever more effective. Just as we train ourselves to run faster and jump higher, we can enhance all our sensory and nonsensory abilities and be stronger for it. After all, this is the basis of much Eastern philosophy, and both yogis and martial arts experts have shown us how effective it can be.

Eastern mysticism also shows us how no one part of human consciousness should always be in exclusive control. It is better that we develop holistic awareness and unity of consciousness to the greatest degree possible. This is never fully achieved, for at various times either the mind, body or base soul may determine the most pressing needs. Even then, no one element of the human organism is ever in total control at any give time. Control is relative to the strengths of the various elements interacting at that timeless instant we call the present. Our actions are forged from these three primary elements acting as much in concert as in isolation. Each has its own physical needs, and each tries to impose them on the overall activity of the entity. As mystics point out, you can control their interaction, balancing one desire or need against others, and moderating any that get out of hand.

The symbiosis of the body, soul and mind is only ended at the death of the flesh. The Spirit and base soul then leave the flesh, transposing their existence to the Afterlife, and the corporeal body decomposes. Death, the great reaper of men, is really a reaper of flesh. The symbiosis between mind and base soul is then strengthened, the mind being systematically absorbed—or consolidated—into the energy of the base soul. There is a physical transformation of the life-energy of the Spirit into soul-energy. Soul-energy, which is the type of energy constructing the base soul, is a stabilized life-energy.

This stabilization occurs according to the natural processes of the Afterlife. Part of the consolidation process is that the life-experiences of the incarnation are integrated with the general pool of experiences and memories of the soul. When consolidation is complete, the soul is a single, integrated entity. The Spirit, as a secondary energy body, is completely absorbed and no longer exists. The soul is at that point physically able to join another fetus, though it usually waits a while. As well as the physical process of consolidation, it must also observe the necessity of planning for the next incarnation.

This means the base soul for your current incarnation is really the base soul and Spirit of your preceding incarnation merged into one coherent entity. This process is reincarnation, and is the process by which souls evolve. Other lifeforms have their own patterns of evolution, but all are in many ways similar to that of souls.

Although a transitory vehicle, the biological organism has a substantial influence on the evolution of the soul. It not only determines the abilities of a given incarnation, but also directly influences the actual construction of soul-energy. The corporeal body is basically a machine that transforms certain food energies into life-energy. Life-energy is in turn transformed into soul-energy. The soul then not only survives, but actually grows. Through consolidation, the sensory experiences of the body, stored first as memories in the life-energy of the Spirit, are eventually fixed in the energy of the soul. Successes and failures in any incarnation determine the soul's priorities for its next incarnation: opportunities seized may open up whole new avenues of evolution; opportunities lost may close the door to certain potential experiences forever. In no small way, what happens while the soul is in flesh determines the course of its future evolution. At the very least, each incarnation yields new experiences and refreshes the soul.

While joined with a corporeal body, the base soul and Spirit conform to its shape. The base soul never leaves the flesh until death, but the Spirit is able to leave on occasion for short durations, a process called astral projection. During astral projection, the Spirit body leaves the corporeal body, but the base soul remains. The Spirit is more mobile because it is not fused with the atoms of the flesh as the base soul is. (This fusing is not something that is detectable by current technology, although it could be detected if appropriate devices were developed. The soul is a physical entity and interacts with the atoms of the body in a very direct way.)

The creation of life-energy involves electromagnetism—a property we associate with atomical structures—and other forces that are interactive with external planes. The life-energy of the Spirit is a bridge between the soul-energy of the base soul and the biological make-up of the corporeal body. The corporeal organism manufactures the life-energy from simple energies derived from food. This life-energy is eventually converted into soul-energy through consolidation in the Afterlife. This is a very ordinary process common to many living entities. In fact, the manufacture of life-energy in one way or another is common to all lifeforms; each lifeform has its own specific vehicles and patterns of growth. It just happens that our specific circumstances involve human biology on this plane as well as the processes of the Afterlife.

Constructing complex life-energies from simple energies is similar in principle to forming biological compounds through biochemistry. The chemistry of the soul, if you will, is such that nonliving energy (in our case, derived from foods, or in the case of plants, light energy from the sun) is formed into life-energy. The transformation is similar to many natural transformations of simple energies we witness daily, such as burning fuel, generating electricity, and so on. Science is also aware of many interactions of energy at the subatomic level that are very close to the process of life-energy manufacture. All such processes are just manifestations of the overall symmetry and unity of nature.

The creation of life-energy is certainly no magical process. Life uses whatever energy is available. In our plane, light energy is our ultimate fuel. If plants didn't use photosynthesis to convert light energy into life, we wouldn't be here. Our bodies only continue a process that plants begin. And the consolidation of life-energy into soul-energy just carries that process one step further. On other planes, lifeforms use other energies, but essentially follow a similar pattern. Simple energies are used to create complex energies, and eventually the right combinations and permutations are achieved to support consciousness. Originally, this process was initiated accidentally. Now it occurs deliberately, but still occurs according to very natural physical processes. In fact, as far as life is concerned, the source of energy is irrelevant, as long as it can be manipulated into the correct configurations. The source is important only insofar as it determines *how* the entity must evolve to use it. Lifeforms do have preferences, just as animals in our world often choose different sources of protein. In broad terms, however, life-energy bodies such as the Spirit and the base soul reconstruct specific energies much as our corporeal bodies reconstruct animal and plant proteins.

The properties of life—consciousness, self-direction, and self-knowledge—are as much the products of the physical environment as are rocks and trees. In our particular sphere of activity, we have become very interested in studying these characteristics of consciousness as well as our external environment. Our quest is two-fold: knowledge of self, and knowledge of environment. This quest is naturally focused on the most obvious elements of our selves and our environment. At the mental level, we focus on our atomical world and on our waking consciousness. Yet at the base levels of consciousness we can perceive a much greater portion of both our environment and our own selves.

We can learn more about ourselves by delving into the abilities of the base soul, if we are able, and by being more conscious of what our own waking minds can achieve. The mind is not an isolated entity; it is linked to other levels of consciousness and even to other levels of physical reality. We can draw on the abilities of our own minds, our own souls, and our guides. Although there are physical reasons why we cannot achieve complete awareness of other planes and our total consciousness, we can always *improve* on the awareness we have at any given time. Then we can have a greater paradigm of not just our own consciousness, but of our total environment.

The Chapter Six
THE AFTERLIFE

It is nearly universal human belief that there is life after the death of the flesh. Every human society has evolved such belief; most people today still believe the soul survives bodily death. It is only in very recent years (primarily this century) and in the industrialized nations that resistance to such belief has formed.

If we are to seek out the true nature and substance of life, we must be aware of the soul. We may prefer to scrap the word soul and develop new terms, but we cannot avoid talking about the entity that gives us life. If we prefer the Jungian terms of "unconscious", "ego", and so on, so be it. We are still talking about the soul, a unit of consciousness far more aware than the human mind that imposes the definitions. The mind is just a skin of consciousness over a great awareness, a skim of ice on a deep lake. This awareness survives the death of the corporeal body in organized form, regardless of the temporal beliefs held in corporeal life.

We can only speculate as to what that survival may be like. This speculation can be based on several legitimate sources of data. Unfortunately, none provide the conclusive evidence the skeptic seeks. For tens of thousands of years, man has held beliefs in the Afterlife. Most societies have been built around such beliefs, the passing on from life on this plane something expected and treated with reverence. Now, we tend to view it with fear or ignore it altogether until it charges into our lives through the death of a loved one. Sooner or later, we all face death. Sooner or later, we all must decide how we view man's spiritual quest for the Afterlife.

If we wonder about the nature of the Afterlife—a perfectly natural thing to do—we are not totally in the dark. Because of our rich heritage of religious and mythological accounts of the Afterlife, we have a ready source of information about what it may be like. Man's written accounts of the Afterlife all have a lot in common. There are significant differences as well, but sufficient similarities exist that we can be certain of at least a few key features of the discarnate state.

There is no one religion or belief that paints a full and complete picture of our Afterlife. The Afterlife is a very complicated plane shared by all souls of our world. This includes animal souls as well as human souls. Although some traditions would have us only consider human beings as "special" enough to have souls, this is not the case.

We are no more special than any other lifeform. We are just one of many, fulfilling a particular niche in a very broad natural environment. This does not mean our holy ideas are to be any less revered; it only means we should not revere ourselves quite so much.

Constructing a composite view of the Afterlife takes a very wide reading of human spiritual tradition and heritage. The Bible offers much, as does the Tibetan Book of the Dead. Homer's Odyssey describes in mythological terms the ancient Greek view of the Afterlife, or more specifically, the Underworld. The legends and myths of the natives of the Americas, Africa and Australia are strikingly similar in their content; the Eastern traditions from Shintoism in Japan to Hinduism in India all offer insight. The traditions all convey aspects of the truth. No one is complete, and no one is totally wrong. And we should always bear in mind that these traditions are transliterations of beliefs emerging in our intellectually dominated plane from a base of consciousness that must strain to pass on to our level of awareness its own inherent truths.

When we consider all these human traditions, we will eventually draw the conclusion that the Afterlife is a place of hope and happiness more than despair. Although there can be negative elements to life-after-death, the awful images of Hell conjured by some Christian traditions are far off the mark. The permanent damnation depicted in Protestantism is simply not a factor in the life after. Even the concept of redemption through Purgatory expressed in Catholicism falls short of reality. No soul is punished except by its own regret; no soul is forced to suffer cruel and unusual punishments beyond those imposed by its own actions. Unfortunately, however, if you believe strongly enough in Hell, you can do a lot to create for yourself your own personal Hell after death. But you can do that in terrestrial life, as well.

For the most part, however, the Afterlife is a place of rest, consolidation and contemplation. The soul can cavort there if it wishes, or rest quietly while preparing for another incarnation on this earth. Its pursuits are of its own choosing, making for a place of happiness and freedom for most souls. Again, happiness in the Afterlife is the choice of the individual, just as happiness in this life is the choice of the individual.

In constructing our composite view of the Afterlife, we must pay close attention to our own internal sense of rhythm and "rightness". As we study the works of ancient and even modern man, we will read passages that feel right. It feels right because it sits well with our own internal consciousness, the various levels of consciousness feeling in harmony with the passage. This feeling does not mean you have encountered "Truth", with a capital "T", but does indicate that you are comfortable with a particular image or impression. It should also mean that the image is close enough to the truth that your internal self is guiding your feeling of satisfaction. As well, you will find that many passages reflect images common to many other texts or descriptions of the life after. These common passages or descriptions, especially if they originate in accounts widely separated in space or time, indicate a common truth.

I believe the similarities of man's various religious and folkloric accounts of the Afterlife are great indicators of their truthfulness, especially when developed independently by many different peoples in many different times. Interestingly enough, many of these similarities also show up in more modern styles of literature and human experience. There are several types of experience, some of which are substantially documented in the formal style of modern scientific and academic research, that support man's traditional reports of the soul's survival of bodily death.

Our only pure perception of the Afterlife occurs when we die. By then it is too late to report effectively to others who are still in flesh. However, there have been many cases of people who have survived the first stages of bodily death who have reported very graphically on what occurs during death. Death is a process by which the soul is levered out of the corporeal body. First to leave is the Spirit, the life-energy structure supporting the consciousness of the mind. This is the mechanism that experiences the out-of-body phenomenon usually reported by people revived from "clinical" death. The Spirit returns, but not until it has glimpsed some of the wonders in store for the departing soul.

There is a common trend in the near-death experience, as it has been dubbed, which includes passage through a tunnel or barrier of light to another world where deceased friends and relatives are waiting to welcome the individual. Sometimes a religious figure or an entity of light is present and asks—verbally or by direct projection of consciousness—whether the individual wishes to stay in this new world or return to the flesh. Many of those who return report they were drawn back by their sense of obligation to their family or an unfinished task, or were sent back by some stronger will. Presumably, those who choose to stay in the new world do not return.

For those who return, the experience is awesome. Many report that their lives change from that point forward, as they attempt to bring new purpose to their endeavors. In addition to the remarkable insights they gain from a personal perspective, their experiences add to man's collective knowledge of the Afterlife. In many ways, these experiences bear out the accounts of our religions and myths. At the very least, they offer subjective evidence that the survival of the soul is not inconceivable.

Considering the possibility that the near-death phenomenon may originate entirely within the brain or mind, psychologists have offered basically two hypotheses. One is that the experience is neurologically driven (originating in the brain), and the second is that it is psychologically driven (originating in the mind). The first hypothesis, even psychologists admit, is weak because no known portion of the brain has been identified to be associated with such experiences. The second hypothesis is also weak, on several counts. It assumes that the individual imagines the event, much as he would in a dream. However, unlike in dreams, the individual is often able to describe upon his revival from death—or near-death—the people, events and conversations that occurred while unconscious or "clinically" dead. Even if the person were merely unconscious, it would not seem likely that an event derived entirely from within his own mind would be able to record the exact words a doctor used while trying to revive him. Also, the descriptions of these experiences hold great similarities across the cultural and philosophical beliefs of the individuals involved. This seems to preclude them from being formed on the basis of preconceptions of the individuals involved. Differences do arise in terms of individual interpretations placed on the events, such as religious people making religious interpretations and nonreligious people making secular interpretations, but the descriptions of the events themselves remain similar. This to me suggests that people make of the events what they will, but the events themselves are an intrinsic part of human life.

The near-death experience has been the subject of several studies and continues to attract a good deal of attention. There are other sources of information about the Afterlife, however, that do not require such risky brinksmanship. Astral projection, for those of us who are able to develop the skill, can allow us to venture to the edges of many worlds, including the Afterlife. Astral projection is essentially a means by which a portion of the consciousness—the same portion that experiences and reports near-death—can leave the body and return. This is the Spirit, the life-energy body associated with the mind.

Dreams are also a valuable source of impressions of other worlds, though it takes some training and experience to learn to dissociate

fact from fantasy. Much of the dream remains fantasy even then, for
dreams are primarily a tool used by our consciousness to work out
experiences of the day in the context of past and future experience.
Still, dreams always provide a wealth of information about the self.

Our best available technique, however, is that of past-life recall.
Past-life recall is a technique for delving into the memories of the
soul. The soul stores all its past lives in its material being, just as we
store the experiences of our current incarnation in the life-energy of
the Spirit. Although some initiation is required to break through the
protective mechanisms of the middle conscious to reach the base
soul's memories, it can be done. Remembering past lives is usually
traumatic at first, because the strongest and most easily retrieved
memories are often those of painful deaths. But a carefully controlled
sequence of past-life recall can also reveal memories of the periods
between lives. This will not only tell you about what the Afterlife is
like, but will tell you what it is like for *you*. This, as we shall see, is a
very critical point.

No matter what we do we will never have a complete picture of the
Afterlife. The Afterlife, like the full awareness of the base soul, is
always shielded from our waking awareness to some degree. Not only
is the barrier between the base soul and mind a blocking factor in
our awareness of the Afterlife, but we must also deal with long-held
ideas of the Afterlife. In the final analysis, no matter what we learn
through books or mysticism, we may not want to relinquish ideas we
have been taught since we were little children.

Few of us really challenge the ideas given us as children; if taught
that the soul is real and goes to Heaven after death we usually accept
that. If taught that the soul is just a euphemism for intangible qualities
of consciousness, we grow up believing the soul is intangible. It is
easiest to accept the beliefs of our parent society, whether religious
or secular. In nature, the course of least resistance is the one most
often followed. In our modern world, the secular view is at war with
the religious view, within individuals as much as between individuals.
Our need to believe in *something* is obvious; in recent years, we have
become less and less certain of exactly what and how to believe.

This uncertainty is mostly the product of our inability to clearly
focus on other planes, including the Afterlife, while in flesh. Much
of our ability to perceive our environment is lost when we join the
flesh. The simple physical reality of our being is that a fragile human
mind cannot tolerate the holistic perceptions available to the base
soul. Such perception would overwhelm the individual's sense of
balance and his ability to assimilate the unceasing in-rush of data. It

is a matter of survival that we exclude the base soul's awareness from our waking awareness. Unfortunately, this has the price of giving our minds only second-hand knowledge of a major portion of our lives: the period we spend in the Afterlife, preparing for our next incarnation.

If you think of the Afterlife, what comes to mind? Perhaps you think of a walled city, where a keeper minds the gate. Perhaps you think of fields of flowers, limpid lakes in the background. Or you might even think of hallowed halls of study, where eager students learn of the inner workings of mysterious forces. Whatever your personal view of the Afterlife, it will be colored to a large degree by your everyday experiences here. Our waking consciousness is predominantly ordered along terrestrial lines. Anything we imagine the Afterlife to be, regardless of how well it is described, is still interpreted according to our terrestrial experience. If we transcribe a description through automatic writing or travel to the Afterlife through astral projection, we will still interpret the events according to terrestrial experience. If we read about or even experience religious revelation about the Afterlife, we are again eventually forced to deal with it in terms familiar to our waking consciousness. It may be unfortunate, but our waking minds are indelibly stamped with the experience of the terrestrial world. Complete knowledge of the Afterlife is beyond us, even when we are discarnate.

Having said that, we can still enlist the aid of guides to help us understand what the Afterlife is really like. We can experiment with various techniques of mediumship—I favor automatic writing—to contact either the souls of the Afterlife or our personal guides. Even with these aids, the most powerful tool at our disposal is imagination, for that is what will stretch the mind to accept the realities of what is to us a foreign world. It is only our imagination that will enable us to delve into our terrestrial experiences and find the elements of it that most closely approximate or are suggestive of elements of the Afterlife. When we have followed all these techniques, we will probably find the Afterlife to appear to us somewhat as follows.

The Afterlife is a plane shared by the souls of all animals of this plane. It serves our world because the soul-entities of this world have been able to exploit certain physical features of a "bridge" or sub-plane. This is a portion of the physical spectrum of this planet that lies between two full-fledged planes. This atomical plane, for example, is a full plane. Within the physical framework of the Afterlife, souls forge common "pockets", or specialized areas, where they can share experiences according to their soul-race and soul-order. The souls of the Human Race, therefore, associate in the Afterlife primarily with other souls of this race, and less so with soul-races of, say, other mammalian species. The classification of souls (the subject of a future book) loosely follows the classifications of biological species, with mammalian species hosting a specific soul-order in which the Human Race is one of a number of soul-races.

Once in the Afterlife, the terms of life are very different than in the incarnate state. Picture, if you can, what it would be like without your biological body. Your consciousness would remain much the same, but your perceptions would suddenly be completely different. You would not perceive through your eyes, nose, skin and so on, but holistically, by "reading" energy patterns directly from objects and other living beings. There are no sensations in the corporeal sense; these remain memories, which you could dust off and recall again if you so chose. By combining and reshaping these memories, you could construct virtually any experience you wanted, much as you daydream now. For instance, you could imagine what it would feel like to stand under a waterfall by picturing in your mind a waterfall and remembering the sensation of water passing over your flesh. But in not having flesh, and not having access to waterfalls (which belong to the atomical world), you would not truly be able to experience the feeling of standing under a waterfall. You would only simulate it. Life in the Afterlife involves much of such simulation. The "real" experiences of the Afterlife, if you want to call them that, involve extending the consciousness to other planes.

When discarnate, the soul draws on its memories of terrestrial life to recreate the best of its past lives. This means that in the Afterlife the soul can create its own version of heaven if it desires, or a plain life that merely mirrors life in flesh. Whatever the soul envisions an ideal life to be, it has the freedom in the Afterlife to go about creating and living that life for as long as it desires. It can also change its circumstances virtually at will. If other souls are to be included in these circumstances, they can share in them according to their own desires.

The Afterlife, within the context of its physical framework, is largely a consciousness-based plane. This is a different sort of reality than, say, our terrestrial plane or even the worlds of our guides, which are constructed primarily of nonliving materials—atoms, in the case of our world. The mechanics of the Afterlife are largely derived from the living entities associated with it. It is therefore quite subjective in form and content, whereas the atomical plane and other planes such as those of our guides are derived from nonliving mechanical processes that are highly objective.

In our plane, for instance, the mechanics of atomics do not change to any great degree because of the way we think (although the mind *can* act on atomical matter in very local circumstances). In the Afterlife, physical reality can be very easily changed by thought. The Afterlife, in effect, takes much of its internal organization from the activity of the souls resident there. This pattern is not unique to animal life, as plant life follows a similar pattern. However, the organization of plant consciousness is significantly different than that of animals.

Soul-entities on other planes also have similar "binary" lifestyles that involve an Afterlife as well as an incarnational world. One world you might describe as an "objective" world for physical evolution, supported by a "subjective" Afterlife as a place of reflection and consolidation.

Souls in the discarnate state have remarkable abilities of convergence and cooperation of consciousness. Cooperatively or singly, they can create through imagination and will almost any type of world they choose. This, of course, is not quite as "real" (or immutable, to be more precise) as our terrestrial world. In these terms, the Afterlife can be a true fantasy land for those who want fantasy, but it is primarily a mechanism for learning of the self. Conversely, the atomical plane (for us and the other lifeforms of terrestrial earth) and other full planes (for the lifeforms there) are primarily mechanisms for learning of the environment. Through cyclical reincarnation, souls gradually integrate more and more experience of the physical environment into their memories. In a way, memory is a mechanism for integrating what is external into the internal self.

While discarnate, the soul can easily view life on various planes. No lifeform can see all existence, but the configuration of energy matter in the human soul enables it to see quite effectively into several planes. One, of course, is this atomical plane, which means that discarnate souls can actually watch what goes on here. Usually, attention is reserved for special friends and relatives (both terms having broader application in the soul-world than here), and major historical events, such as a war or cataclysmic natural disaster. The soul also has friends and relatives on other physical planes, where they may be discarnate or pursuing incarnational experiences in terms suitable to their host plane. These planes have a peripheral role to play in our evolution.

The souls of terrestrial earth (those in flesh) have little need to occupy themselves with inter-plane observation. However, they do so at a base level of consciousness that helps to engineer day-to-day events. This activity is not usually apparent to the mind, which functions in virtual isolation. While out of flesh, however, the soul takes advantage of its vantage point to assess potential interactions between planes, future events that are clearly predictable, and the soul's own hopes for personal achievement. To use a military analogy, the souls in flesh are engaged in tactical planning, whereas the souls out of flesh are engaged in strategic planning.

Thus, plans made in the Afterlife are forming a context in which the activities of a single incarnation in flesh will play a part. Not least of these plans are those that are made in accordance with the wishes and aspirations of other souls, both of our race and others. Life, afterall, is a cooperative venture. Experiences can be planned or they can be left to chance, but as the soul evolves, it increasingly realizes that there is more value and satisfaction in planned experiences than in those that simply happen.

It is difficult to describe the shift of awareness from the atomical plane to the Afterlife without using spatial concepts. Perhaps it is sufficient to say that the soul in aggregate at death shifts its orientation from a three-dimensional world to a non-three-dimensional world, while maintaining many perceptions in three dimensions. Whereas the soul in the Afterlife has no *physically* generated need to view existence in three dimensions, it retains a *psychical* desire to do so simply because this is convenient and familiar. Yet in the discarnate state, psychology becomes a force of much greater proportions than we credit it here; the environment of the discarnate soul is almost purely psychical.

When the base soul is completely removed from the flesh, there is no turning back. The biological organism dies. For a while, traces of life-energy linger in the organism, but this is residue of a living process now defunct. The organized structures of life-energy, the base soul and Spirit, reform their collective existence in the Afterlife without the corporeal organism. Remember that the Spirit is first formed by the interaction of a soul joining a corporeal organism in the womb. When the base soul and Spirit separate from the flesh, they immediately transfer their physical consciousness to the Afterlife—much like flipping over a coin. Once in the Afterlife, they are melded into one consciousness, and a physical fusing—consolidation—begins.

The Afterlife provides a temporary suspension of material involvement that is a needed rest for the soul. In the Afterlife, the soul is not so much at the mercy of unforgiving environmental forces. It lives in a freer environment, one established by the collective consciousness of related souls. In our world we must expend great amounts of energy in the care and manipulation of our corporeal bodies. Inevitably, the body fails. The aging process can be debilitating for the soul as well as the body, and the Afterlife provides a needed respite from the ongoing struggle to maintain and improve corporeal existence.

Although the period spent in the Afterlife has specific physical roles to play in the evolution of the soul, it can be viewed to some degree as a holiday from the flesh. There, the soul can create a world of its own choosing. It can live out many approaches to a problem before committing itself to a single approach that will stamp itself into the blueprint of a terrestrial incarnation. Actions in the Afterlife are like taping and retaping an audio tape in a recording studio: sooner or later a recording must be presented to the market, and sooner or later a soul must put its plans into effect in the terrestrial world. In working out problems and planning for the future, the soul can create a world of its own choosing, a place where it can simulate events of the future or recreate events of the past. It can even join in what is happening on the earth plane at this very moment, though terrestrials often ignore the discarnates around them.

The soul has more freedom in the Afterlife than terrestrial life allows. Unfortunately, the Afterlife has limitations too. Out of flesh, the soul cannot gather new materials for its growth. It needs the material composition of a plane such as terrestrial earth for the manufacture of life-energy. Into this life-energy will be stamped the memories of the new incarnation, memories of events that were planned and rehearsed in the Afterlife. When these memories are formed in terrestrial life, they seem new; in actuality, they are the playing out of roles established in the Afterlife. The success of the soul in concluding the events of the terrestrial incarnation is never totally certain. Much can change, and much can be misconstrued.

The soul's behavior, even in the Afterlife, is largely molded by its experiences on the terrestrial plane. Both our biological and cultural evolution have reinforced this trait. The soul, in effect, *is* its terrestrial experience, even though it has abilities resident within itself that are poorly executed on the terrestrial plane. We often carry our desires of the flesh and our terrestrial incarnations into the Afterlife; if the desires are too strong, the soul may get transfixed in a state not fully cognizant of either plane. This is the state of the wandering soul, one that, happily, corrects itself in time. On the whole, however, the newly departed soul soon occupies itself in the Afterlife, using its creative potentials to remake its life a little closer to its own personal ideals, even if only for a little while.

The purpose of the Afterlife is to plan for future incarnations. These plans do not really fit our terrestrial ideas of planning, but encompass a much broader scope. For instance, we may view a baby's death as a tragedy, but the soul may only be joining the body for a short while for a specific reason of its own choosing. The briefest terrestrial incarnation can enhance the soul's evolution. Changing any evolutionary process is analogous to turning an ocean liner under full power; much effort and time is required, as the stage for change must first be set. In the Afterlife, plans are made, options explored, a course set, and finally events are put in motion.

The soul's plans and objectives are necessarily oriented to what is available to that soul. There are many courses available at any given time, and many potential decisions that can be made. There are, however, limits to these choices. To move from one point to another in life first requires preparation. A surgeon cannot simply cease being a surgeon and take up carpentry. In spite of his long training to become a surgeon, he must begin a new and different apprenticeship to become a carpenter. The success of his transformation even then depends on his innate skills.

Likewise for the soul. The soul cannot become something different simply by wanting to. It must evolve. Its chances for success depend on first the reasonableness of the expectation, then on the acuity, intelligence, and perseverence with which it pursues the goal. In human terms, the goals of the soul must for the most part be fulfilled through the medium of human flesh. What cannot be achieved through human flesh must wait until the soul can proceed in a new direction. Like turning the ocean liner, this takes more than just stating the wish. The correct mechanisms must be put in motion, and time must pass.

The soul makes its decisions as to the general course of its evolution in the Afterlife. It decides what it wants to do, and how to go about doing it. It then awaits an appropriate vehicle. This vehicle is a fetus, never perfect for the task, but the choice is made on the best chances for success. When the soul commits itself to joining a particular fetus, a course has been set.

The events that follow are largely foreshadowed, if not predicted outright. At the same time, however, surprises can intervene. Like the Titanic, heralded as unsinkable, the most certain course can take a tragic turn—if the parties involved fail to perceive an obvious risk. Although at times a relatively simple decision can effect a dramatic change in evolution, the stage has inevitably been set by a long period of prior evolution. Again in human terms, a dramatic change is the result of many years of effort, and likely many incarnations concentrated on that purpose.

In a very real sense, the human soul is committed to evolving within human bodies. Its course is set. Though the course will evolve daily, dramatic changes require preparation. Before joining higher levels of experience, we must complete our experience here. This means becoming fully and totally involved in the physical realities of this plane.

In a way, our concentration on the properties of terrestrial earth is the logical outgrowth of our dependence on these properties. While we live here, we must be responsive to the conditions here. We cannot simply cease our relationship with this plane; we have to return here again and again, slowly building the energies and experience we need to join higher planes. To a large extent this is a simple physical process, analogous to nuclear reactions that can change one atomic element into another. In addition, we require experience to prepare us for the kind of life we will have to adapt to in a new physical environment.

In the meantime, we evolve here. The soul guides our waking experience as a blind man uses a cane. It knows the route it wishes to follow and what lies in its path. It uses the body to "feel" its way; by joining human flesh, the awareness of the soul is submerged beneath the sensory awareness of the corporeal body. In the waking world, the organic senses are the primary mechanism for deriving experience, and the soul must bide by that fact.

That fact does not mean the soul is powerless. The soul instills desire in the organism to achieve higher ideals and purpose. Though biological needs may consume us at times, the soul accepts this as part of the price of experience. The wise soul even turns these biological needs to higher purpose, using them as motivating forces to achieve personal goals. Such goals may be a good family life, which can enhance the growth of the individual, or some career that benefits others. These goals can be fully expressed in the Afterlife in many ways before being implemented in a terrestrial incarnation.

Before a soul joins a body, it analyzes the advantages and disadvantages of the chosen body. It knows in general terms how successful it will be in that incarnation based on its assessment of the practical limitations of the vehicle, the time in history, and concurrent social and environmental conditions. The soul can judge the value of its many possible futures as quickly as we can call to mind an event from yesterday. It is like looking at a road map and actually seeing the scenery you will see as you drive. Not every event is certain, nor can every event be controlled. But the developing skills and knowledge of the soul enable it to get better and better at predicting its own future, and determining what its future will be.

Because of the soul's abilities of prediction, the future is usually no surprise at the base levels of consciousness. It is the mind that views the future with such foreboding, wonder, and curiosity. Our mental existence while in flesh is like having a curtain drawn around the major portion of our consciousness, the mind blindfolded by the corporeal body. The ability of the mind to perceive the true nature of its existence depends on how clearly the base soul can interact with the mind through the medium of the flesh. For most of us, this interaction does not result in a very clear perception.

The mind is a new entity in each incarnation, a blank slate to be filled with experiences. It is a mechanism for exploration and discovery, and helps the individual to overcome the weaknesses of prior incarnations. When the incarnation is over, the base soul and the Spirit leave the flesh. The successes and failures of that incarnation are then measured against the soul's prior expectations. At the same time, the life-energy of the Spirit is incorporated into the base soul. The consciousness of the soul is unified once more.

After many such reincarnations, the soul is eventually ready for a new type of evolution. It achieves a state in which it can begin to use a higher plane as its focus of evolution. It will then cease to reincarnate on this terrestrial earth. The conditions it will find in this new plane will be somewhat like those of the Afterlife, because the souls in the Afterlife also draw on other planes when constructing their trial experiences. The Afterlife, then, is as much a place for learning as is our terrestrial world. For us, it is the first place we learn of all the planes of Earth.

Chapter Seven
THE ATOMICAL PLANE

The atomical plane is all that is encompassed by space. In fact, the spacetime system described in Einsteinian physics is virtually synonymous with what souls call the atomical plane. This parallel is no accident. Both the language of physics and the language of souls are attempting to define a major aspect of human experience. This is our experience of terrestrial earth and the cosmos in which it exists.

Astronomy has shown us how vast the atomical plane is. We exist in a cosmic ocean so huge that it defies comprehension. As I write this, astronomers have just announced the discovery of a galaxy some 44 billion light-years away. This discovery is not the last that will be made, for no one knows how wide space really is or how far human technology can some day be stretched. Yet for the time being 44 billion light-years—a light-year being some six million million miles of space— is sufficient to overwhelm the imagination.

Space is only half of the equation of the cosmos. Time is the other half. The interaction of time and space goes far beyond human conception, though once again, Einsteinian physics points us to inescapable conclusions. We know that time is not a constant force, that space can alter time, and that time can alter space. Through the lifetime of the cosmos, space has expanded from an infinitesimally small point (a singularity) to its present size and expands still. This expansion is an expansion of the atomical plane.

The fact that space is expanding leads us to believe that there is an edge to space. While the edge of space certainly does not have qualities that are shared by, say, the edge of a razor, there is undoubtedly some validity to the concept of an edge of space. There are limits to all things within the universe. Similarly, our perception of a linear passage of time leads us to believe there may be an end to time. As a spacetime system, then, the cosmos definitely has limits. The question is what lies beyond those limits. If we accept that a finite system is not necessarily a closed system, we must assume that the edge of space, the end of time, and any other limits the cosmos may have are portals to new systems beyond a spacetime framework.

The cosmos, in reality, is a system interleaved with other systems. Our sciences are perhaps too young to delve into the reality of our neighboring systems, but the fact that the soul uses both the atomical plane and others for its evolution gives us some insight as to the directions our sciences may someday lead us. The atomical plane is just one plane among many. It derives its being from a complete spectrum of physical energies that can be divided into many major and minor scales. This spectrum forms the total being of our planet Earth and all the other material bodies of the cosmos. And even this broader scale is representative of only one small portion of the total potential creativity of the universal force.

When the cosmos exploded into being, the creative forces unleashed did not just create stars, planets, moons, comets, and other galactic bodies. A mechanism was put in place by which secondary planes could form around any atomical body that was created. This means that the atomical plane has a special ability to spawn secondary planes according to specific forces associated with atoms. This plane provides a base from which other planes can evolve, then acts as an anchor for their continued existence. This means any single atom or collection of atoms can have associated with it many alternate systems. These secondary planes can be viewed as part of a single system that includes our atomical plane, or as systems in their own right.

The secondary planes exist within a context largely determined by the fundamental properties of the atomical plane. In these terms, "secondary" does not imply secondary importance, but only an order of configuration. Because other worlds are derived from primary atomical worlds such as our terrestrial earth, souls often refer to the atomical plane as the base plane.

This property as a base or anchor does not mean the atomical energies of our plane hold exclusive sway over any other plane. It merely means that in the local architecture, energies are largely configured according to rules initiated in atomical energies. Atomical energies are any energies specifically associated with atoms—the material energies of atoms, if you will. When the Big Bang occurred, the stage was set not just for the creation of an atomical cosmos such as we can view with our telescopes, but also many other layers of physical reality. In perceiving only the atomical plane, we are perceiving only a very limited portion of material reality.

The simultaneous existence of the various planes is possible because of the great—but not unlimited—cohesive power of atoms. Atoms are extremely cohesive constructions of energy. As well as binding energy in their own internal matrixes, they allow other external energies to bind to them. These other energies are sufficiently similar to base atomical energies to enable them to interact directly, but also sufficiently different so they can retain a separate existence within a common spectrum. The atomical plane is much like a mother who gives birth to a number of children, but allows them to achieve an identity of their own within the family unit. Interestingly, the secondary planes evolve in association with specific collections of atoms. A planet, such as ours, can have secondary planes, but these planes do not extend through space the way, say, light energy does. A secondary plane, even in its local context, cannot be said to occupy space, even though its parent body does.

This may at first seem confusing, especially considering how dependent we are on our three-dimensional point of view. However, if we can set aside this point of view for a moment, the picture should emerge more clearly. Remember that space is a concept derived from the dimensions of height, width, and depth. These dimensions are only valid while considered in a spatial system. A secondary plane associated with a three-dimensional body is not required to share the dimensional characteristics of its parent body. In other words, a spatial construct can spawn nonspatial constructs; a system in which space is a predominant characteristic can give birth to systems in which other characteristics predominate. And even though you cannot see the secondary system, it may still be very closely associated with the parent body. Its association is not organized in spatial terms, but in terms of interactive forces. It is "concurrent" with the parent body, as opposed to "colocated".

Although science has not yet developed a theory of coexistent planes exactly as I am stating it here, there are similar ideas in official scientific circles. A suggestive theory in modern physics argues for 11 dimensions within the cosmos, based on natural symmetries of subatomic particles. Seven of these dimensions are assumed to be undetectable in our terms, while four (the three of space and one of time) are quite familiar in everyday terms. The seven extra dimensions are useful in solving certain problems that exist in rationalizing subatomic behavior. Similar theories call for various other numbers of dimensions. These theories, whether right or wrong, reveal a very interesting fact: to rationalize all that we currently know, we are forced to acknowledge gaps in our knowledge. These gaps indicate that there may indeed be parallel realities we can't detect with our corporeal senses or atomical devices. This, in fact, is exactly what my guides hope to convey through this book.

My guides indicate that there are some 21 planes associated with the planet Earth, with a number of other subplanes, or bridges, interposed between the planes. The planes are arranged along a continuum of matter-energies, each plane formed on the basis of a particular base energy form. Atomical energy, as one base energy, forms also the base for the entire matter-energy spectrum. Other secondary base energies are derived from the primary base. The order of configuration is simply a result of physical processes that have culminated in the very complex entity that is our planet. Other atomical bodies, such as a simple collection of inert gases floating through space, do not have as complex a set of secondary planes as an active planet such as Earth.

Here again I should mention that the capitalized "E" of Earth indicates the entire planet, including all its planes. Terrestrial earth, with a small "e", earns its name because of its properties as the base plane for the planet as a whole. But the key thing to remember is that while the cosmos is a single unified system from here to galaxies 44 billion light-years away and beyond, each secondary plane is associated with a single atomical body. Where there is a collection of atoms congealed in a single entity, such as a planet or other body, secondary planes may form. The order and complexity of the formation of secondary planes is entirely dependent on the forces that have acted on that atomical body in the past and that are acting on it now.

As it happens, the complex atomical structure of terrestrial earth, its ideal orbit around the sun, and its own internal nuclear, chemical and electromagnetic activity all combine to form a very dynamic environment for the evolution of secondary planes. Life, for example, does not necessarily evolve on an atomical body; it may, however, exist on secondary planes while the terrestrial plane of that atomical body remains barren. It happens that our planet supports life both on this plane and others, and that life is continuously upgrading this entire planet as an evolutionary entity.

The formation of secondary planes does follow distinct patterns, some of which are more conducive to the evolution of life than others. There are patterns in all behavior within the universe, and our part of it is no exception. Although we cannot know in detail what is going on at the far ends of the cosmos, we can be certain that an atom there is subject to the same physical laws as an atom here. The basic forces of the atom are consistent throughout the cosmos. Similarly, the forces that generate secondary planes from the matter of atoms (or atomical energy) are also consistent throughout the cosmos. Special events occur periodically according to special sequences or combinations of forces, but these also occur according to strict rules of behavior. Exploding stars (supernovae), black holes (collapsed stars), and pulsars (stars that emit radio energies) are just a few special events that stand out on a cosmic scale. So is the evolution of life.

Life is a product of the entire cosmic experience. This includes the activity of secondary planes as well as our atomical plane. Life, contrary to current scientific theory, did not originate in the primordial soup of the early terrestrial oceans, but on another plane. Having evolved on another plane, certain types of primitive life-energies were able to make a transition to inhabit the near-organic molecules that evolved in the early seas of earth. The spark of life that is missing in evolutionary theory is present still in our very being; our life-energy, though using atomical energies as a source of material being, is nonetheless an offshoot of a life-energy that originated on a secondary plane.

Life is actually a complex configuration of material energies. These energies require a greater degree of processing than is possible within an exclusively atomical environment such as our terrestrial earth; consequently, lifeforms that use this plane also require periodic consolidation phases in an Afterlife. The corporeal body, in effect, is an atomical agent that is imbued with life through a two-pronged evolutionary heritage. The first agent is indeed the chemical fires of early earth. In the violence of the cooling earth, certain compounds of hydrogen, carbon and oxygen began to form according to very natural atomical processes. These processes have been duplicated to some extent in labs that have produced what scientists call nonbiogenic organic molecules, meaning organic compounds such as amino acids produced by nonbiological processes. Similar compounds have been found in meteorites, demonstrating that such processes are not unique to Earth.

Although these compounds could never on their own make the leap from near-organic substances to the truly organic—that is, spontaneously imbue themselves with life—they provided a medium that could support equally primitive near-life energies. These near-life energies developed in their own context on secondary planes and somehow found it possible to join in the development of near-organic molecules on this plane. Eventually, presumably over millions of years, this process induced true life in biological entities, life being defined as something with some modicum of self-direction and self-sustenance.

The ability of certain secondary planes to originate independent life-energies is not dissimilar to the ability of our plane to create more atoms. Atoms are created and destroyed continuously. Any atom has a certain lifespan, in which it will decay into its component energies. Some of these are relatively rapid and others occur only after many millions of years. Life-energies also decay; their existence in coherent energy bodies such as souls is the product of consistent replenishment, much like the replenishment of the biological cells of your corporeal body. In these terms, the energy particles are replaced on a continuing basis, just as the atoms of your flesh are replaced on a continuing basis. The end result is a structure of consciousness that perceives a continuity of awareness, memories and so on, while systematically replacing its actual material composition.

The atomical processes of the corporeal body aid the creation of life-energy. Now that biological life has been established on our plane, it continues of its own momentum. The terms of its survival are quite familiar to us; each organism that currently exists can be traced back through its parental lineage to a simple form of proto-life. All life in our world is directly descended from a single biological source. In that very accurate sense, each human being is very much related to each amoeba. Biological processes have branched out, resulting in significantly different organisms, but their heritage is the same. Differences do emerge between the entities of earth in terms of their life-energies, because here is where a different heritage can take effect.

The souls of the Human Race, for instance, are not as closely related to the life-energy of amoeba as their biological hosts are related to each other. This is because the evolutionary heritage of the soul-races using terrestrial biological species originated in a number of different planes. As life-energy entities, they may not be closely related at all. The life-energy of any living entity, in other words, has its own evolutionary history. Just as biological species each have an evolutionary history, the various soul-races of our world also have their own evolutionary histories.

Further differences emerge in life-energy forms as different patterns of survival established themselves within the respective biological contexts. Each organism fights for its own survival. As each organism tries to eke out its own niche within the environment, it inevitably leads itself to different patterns of behavior. These different patterns of behavior in turn lead to greater differentiations in the actual organism. And so it goes, differentiations eventually resulting in the definition of new species, very much as Darwin described over a century ago. Life, once it gains a toehold, exploits every possible niche in an environment. It necessarily changes itself in the process, resulting in great diversity of lifeforms. This is true not just on our terrestrial plane, but on all planes.

I suspect many of my readers are not yet comfortable with the fact that I have removed the origin of life from terrestrial earth to another plane. It may seem little improvement over the idea of the spontaneous creation of life by some divine power. But we must remember that no one has yet put forward a plausible theory of how biological life can be derived from nonliving processes. It is obvious that life exists, and that it is able to continue itself through various means. Animals give birth and lay eggs, plants sprout offshoots, cast seeds, and root themselves from cuttings. These methods are all tools of existing life. None of them demonstrate how life can be spontaneously generated from nonlife.

The solution I propose is no less credible than molecules spontaneously generating life. I am simply saying that life-energies somehow originated from nonliving energies. The processes by which this happened are not indigenous to this plane, but have become involved with this plane through a systematic process of colonization that is the hallmark of living energies. Life spreads wherever it can. The actual process that created the first life will remain for a time a mystery. I certainly do not know what it is. However, I accept the premise given me by my guides, which is that life-energies originated on planes physically suited to the generation of life-energies from what we may term near-life energies. I have no qualms about accepting this premise because to me it seems eminently reasonable. Like the physicist who decides to postulate another seven dimensions to make more rational sense of the four we empirically know about, I find the idea that life originated on another plane solves a problem that seems hopelessly unresolvable in terrestrial terms.

Even in our terrestrial context, we do not understand the generation of life. We only know that biological bodies in some way allow life to manifest itself within our world. What happens is that life joins specific biological constructs in specific ways. A life-entity, such as a soul, can join a biological organism with which it is compatible. This compatibility is the result of careful preparation and evolution. Nothing in nature happens spontaneously; no lifeform suddenly decides it will change its entire biological context and suddenly does so. Any significant change requires a specific combination and order of events.

The experience of terrestrial earth, then, is an evolutionary process. We are souls inhabiting biological organisms. In doing so, we accept the physical requirements of inhabiting such organisms. We also accept the limitations. We have obviously found this to be to our advantage, or we wouldn't be here. What remains is to explore the specific sequence of events that has led us to our current situation. Our sciences have studied our biological history and have mapped the evolutionary path of our human species. This is one branch of our heritage. The other branch remains to be explored, the heritage of the soul. The soul is equally a product of evolution, though an evolution that is not so tied to this single plane.

The atomical plane is the habitat of the biological organism. The human corporeal organism is an atomical construct, a product of this atomical plane. The soul, however, is not. It originated on another plane, its specific history involving several planes besides terrestrial earth. This soul-history is very much tied to this planet, but is not restricted to terrestrial earth. As far as the soul is concerned, our terrestrial experience is very recent indeed.

Souls progress through various evolutionary phases, gradually becoming more sophisticated as life-entities. All lifeforms evolve from simple lifeforms to increasingly complex lifeforms. Their individual evolution occurs in their own individual terms. Some eventually spend some time using the evolutionary potential of this plane, many others do not. It just happens that our soul-race has evolved in such a way as to lead it to this particular species in this particular time. The souls of our race, in fact, have only been associated with this species since the latter days of Neanderthal Man. Before that, another soul-race guided the species.

In fact, our use of the human species and even our presence on terrestrial earth is quite incidental to the plane's physical role as a bonding agent for other planes. Life is very fluid, moving from plane to plane as it seizes opportunities for self-development. Life uses the physical properties of its environment for, first, its sustenance and, second, its evolution. Once involved with a specific environment, life then becomes a part of that environment, and part of the equation of physical events that guides the environment. As we are learning, even a single lifeform such as man can have a profound influence on the environment. In some planes, life can take an even greater role in shaping the physical events of its habitat.

The role of life is actually even more interactive with the environment than we would think at first glance. Life actually incorporates part of its environment within itself. This is done not only through experience within that environment, but through a physical absorption of certain materials from that environment. This, in fact, is the primary role of the corporeal organism. It actually digests its environment, both in terms of physical perception and the digestion of food. Some of this food is formed into biochemicals to sustain the organism itself, and some of it (specific types of energy) is incorporated into the life-energy of the Spirit. The Spirit is then later transformed into soul-energy. At that point, energy from our terrestrial world, the atomical plane, is transformed into nonatomical energy. A portion of this plane can thus be taken into a higher material plane, either for a brief visit (as souls often do) or for a more lasting relationship. The goal of our soul-race is to eventually evolve beyond the need for further reincarnation on this plane and to join a higher plane for systematic evolution there.

Terrestrial earth, then, is only temporarily our primary habitat. For now it is our home, a resource for the materials and experiences of our lives. It is the focus of our corporeal incarnations and the object of the long-term strategies of the soul. For many of us while we are incarnated in human flesh, terrestrial earth is all that matters.

Our waking awareness is largely bound by the atomical plane. We perceive the atomical cosmos with our telescopes and our naked eyes. Our senses provide a natural focus on what we do here; this is part of our biological arrangement. At the same time, however, we are less aware of alternate realities than we need to be. There are other worlds that interact with ours, worlds that have entities within them that are open to communications with us. Some of these worlds are very close at hand, among them our own Afterlife.

It is somewhat ironic that the very aspects of life that can prove that our environment extends beyond atomical reality are not accepted as proof. This is because the modern industrial cultures that believe in empiricism are so driven by atomical nature that all our tools and devices are atomical. Unfortunately, atomical tools do not serve well to discover aspects of the nonatomical. No device we have can actually measure thought. We do have devices such as electroencephalographs (EEGs) that measure electrical potentials within the brain, which are only the "aftershocks", so to speak, of thought processes. EEGs do not actually measure thought itself.

Neither our machines nor our corporeal bodies are capable of physically measuring nonatomical reality. They are locked in on atomical nature because they are themselves explicitly the product of atomical nature. Our only tools for stepping outside our atomical environment are our own life-energies. And so far, we do not trust our perceptions of other worlds sufficiently to accept them in and of themselves as proof of other worlds. Objective science remains very much atomical science.

There is much human knowledge, however, that is not objective. This knowledge often transcends the dry facts of empirical research and offers our race its highest qualities. Our knowledge of such ideals as honor, justice and, above all, love are things we know without objective evidence. We accept them and know them to exist. These are the ideals of life, and life is something science has not yet succeeded in reducing to objective formula. Whereas science has shown us native relationships between aspects of physical nature, it is the forces of consciousness that show us all that is greatest about life.

The soul is certainly not atomical. At the same time, it requires the atomical plane as a source of raw material and, more specifically, it requires the organic body to transform primary energy forms in this plane to the more complex forms of life-energy. This purpose does not arise from *conscious* demand, but *physical* demand. In a physical sense, green plants need light, animals require protein. Light or protein may or may not convey consciousness as we understand it, but they certainly fuel the *physical* requirements of plants and animals. The need for such fuel exists only because of their physical context.

At the physical level, the soul functions similarly to light-energy, atoms, or any other physical effect within nature. As a lifeform, it has additional requisites. It seeks to off-set its own debilitation through acts of will. This level of behavior is slightly more evolved than simple physical reactivity. However, it is still relatively simple, much the same as a plant turning to face the sun. Both plant and soul seek to survive, nature causing this reaction as certainly as it causes chemical reactions.

At a yet higher level of activity, the soul has unidirectional action on its environment. The soul can actually *decide* upon an action and the environment is forced to react. This is a product of the soul's physical existence as a lifeform. Though guided to a large extent by external forces, the soul indeed has a measure of free will. This free will acts entirely within the framework of nature and is constrained by the physical impositions of its more immediate environment. This environment establishes a context of activity, or a "realm of effect". Man's modern efforts are largely oriented to understanding the physical environment provided by the atomical plane.

That concentration, not surprisingly, leaves us with little knowledge of anything that is not directly related to atoms. To range beyond the nature of atoms is to venture into the subjective—and the subjective is easily dismissed when it doesn't fit accepted theories. The soul is such an event. It doesn't fit the atomical orientation of modern science, though it is very much a part of our realm of effect. In fact, the soul is the epicenter of our realm of effect; only a peculiar blind spot in our terrestrial perception keeps us from studying its role more directly.

We must widen our understanding of our environment before we can understand the soul. Society at large may not be prepared to do this, but our physical realm of effect will continue to center on the soul. Without an appreciation for the potential benefits of such an understanding, there is little likelihood that substantial resources will be devoted to the quest. But for many people, including myself, there are mysteries too immediate and too real to delay a personal investigation. My experiences of precognition, telepathy, mediumship, and out-of-the-body travel are my own personal impetus to investigation. Such mysteries cannot go forever unresolved. Sooner or later some critical mass will be achieved in terms of the people who experience them and have the means to explore them in systematic terms. In time, the unknowable phenomena of today will be known and as much a part of our public education as physics and math are now. In the meantime, our knowledge of nonatomical events will remain only subjectively understood.

The single most important event that will drive this evolving quest is death. Each of us must die. It is a requisite of our biological natures. We must somehow come to terms with this event, and with many of the events that occur in association with death. Most of us do not want to face up to the fact that we must die; psychological trauma is often associated with the passing of a loved one, and people do many reactionary things as they begin to sense their own mortality. An understanding that the death of the body is not the end of consciousness could allay much of this trauma. Death is something that can be prepared for, much as you would prepare for a trip abroad. Like travelling to foreign lands, there is always much that is unknown, but circumstances are bound to be much more pleasant if one is at least minimally prepared.

To understand death requires knowledge of certain nonatomical principles. If we are to understand these principles, we must acknowledge that there are indeed nonatomical events. Rather than focus single-mindedly on atomics, we must open our minds to other planes. We must learn that the atomical plane is only one potential plane among many, and to consider that there may be more to life than the organic processes of the corporeal body.

The atomical plane is no more isolated from other planes than our consciousnesses have made it. We can indeed be aware of other planes and the entities that live there if we choose to. We cannot verify their existence in atomical terms, though this is what our atomical orientation demands. We have evolved a self-deceptive tendency to view our environment only in terms of the atomical forces that form the basis of so much of our experience. And yet we know that there are elements of our experience that systematically defy atomic science. These are the experiences of our souls, the products of the very life-energies that give us consciousness and the ability to perceive the difference between nonliving atomical elements and our own selves. These experiences—as common as everyday thought, as esoteric as past-life recall and mediumship—are the ones that force us in some way or other to acknowledge that we are part of a vaster system than just this atomical cosmos. Though this cosmos is our home and very dear to us, it is not all that exists.

Chapter Eight
THE PLANES OF EARTH

The planet Earth consists of 21 planes. Each of these planes occupies a specific portion of a spectrum of material energy. The material spectrum takes its fundamental unity of organization from the atomical plane, which is why the atomical cosmos is also called the base plane. Atomical bodies provide a base or anchor around which other planes can form.

Our home planet is only one atomical body in the cosmos. The cosmos seethes with activity, and is filled with all manners of atomical forces and energies. We can all witness some of this activity. Stars take form, burn furiously and collapse, heaving enormous amounts of energy across space. Space, though impossibly empty to the naked eye, is actually filled with energy and substance: gravitational fields, radio, heat and other electromagnetic energies, neutrinos, and many other particles such as the so-called "ghost" or virtual particles that glimmer in and out of existence like mirages. The cosmos acts wholly within the bounds of spacetime, but offers creative power to other planes.

The cosmos is a complete, unified system. Every aspect of it interacts with every other aspect. No one planet is separate unto itself, no single star can live or die without having an extraordinary impact on all other bodies in the cosmos. All this activity is bounded by a few key limits. Space is limited in physical terms, as is time. Though the atomical plane is expanding, it expands according to specific limits and rules. It can be presumed to be only so wide at a given time; some astronomers claim to have calculated its current diameter. There are also limits to the expressions of matter and form within the cosmos. Atomical matter cannot surpass the speed of light; all physical activity we understand in scientific terms occurs in a context determined by this special speed. And there are the limits of subdivision of atomical matter itself; at some point, we assume, there is a basic indivisible particle or set of particles that is the root of atomical matter as we know it.

We may ponder the limits of our known cosmos without ever really knowing all about them. We wonder if time began with the Big Bang, if it will end with the Big Crunch. We know there are limits to the cosmos, and wonder what lies beyond. If space can expand, what does it expand into? Does it just fold in on itself as some scientists suggest, or does it have some other mechanism that defines its outer boundaries? If time ends, what measurement marks the passage of what follows? These are the imponderables of our existence, questions we have evolved the sophistication to ask, but not answer. We may assume that some system takes over where this system ends, but our tools and imaginations remain firmly anchored to the perceptions and mechanisms of this one tiny planet in the sea of the cosmos.

In effect, the limits of our knowledge are those imposed by our tools. In these terms, the human body is one of our greatest tools, as is our consciousness. Neither body nor soul can measure the cosmos or its sister systems in their greatest dimensions, nor can any mechanical device we develop. The wonders of the atomical cosmos are so great that there is endless fuel for the wildest fires of speculation. Neither philosopher nor physicist is truly able to paint a picture of the edge of space. Both can only offer the barest inklings of what that edge may be. Though we can list many of the limits of the cosmos and describe their characteristics with great mathematical precision, we cannot easily picture them in the mind's eye. Our powers of cognition are so trained upon the set conditions of this terrestrial earth that we can rarely raise ourselves above our basic animal perceptions. We can view our greatest concepts only in abstract terms, reaching into the fabric of our everyday experience for analogies to describe to ourselves such things as the edge of space.

And yet there are broader terms still in which to view the universe. We have explored the bounds within which atoms must function, but have we even begun to explore the bounds within which consciousness must function? If our powers of cognition are stretched to encompass any genuine understanding of our primary environment, the cosmos, how can we begin to understand how other worlds may exist all about us hidden from our view? Our world is just one of many in a single location in space. The bounds of the cosmos are bridges to other systems, doorways to new experiences of reality that our minds cannot fully grasp. We can discuss notions of parallel worlds, but fail to truly picture them as they exist. We are locked into our peculiar view of material reality.

Such things as the expansion of space seem far less magical if we view them within the context of an open universe. If we could understand how our system, the cosmos, borrows from neighboring systems for its growth, we could begin to appreciate the true expanse of the universe. The material cosmos is just one thin slice or layer of reality. It composes a particular framework within which certain types of behavior are manifested. This cosmos yields a vast array of experience, from biological evolution on terrestrial earth to the explosion of supernovae. Yet the atomical plane also interacts with other planes. These other planes are not evident to our corporeal senses because our corporeal senses are not capable of perceiving them. However, they are evident to our noncorporeal nature, to layers of consciousness that interact with them as readily as our senses of sight, smell, hearing, and so on can perceive aspects of our atomical world.

Because we are accustomed to thinking in spatial terms, we have trouble visualizing how other planes, replete with life, can exist within what we regard as a closed atomical system. We are used to thinking of terrestrial earth as being the whole planet, just as we are used to thinking of the cosmos as the entire universe. But this point of view is something of a self-deception, for we are part of a much greater system that includes more kinds of life than we can ever hope to witness.

It is surprising, even shocking, to consider for the first time that there are living entities all around us that we can't see. In fact, these entities are passing through us, and us through them, even as you read this. They exist in their terms, some of them aware of us but most not. They, like us, are subject to their own limitations, interests, and immediate focus.

The notion of many realities folding into each other within the same finite space is not nearly so staggering if you think of all the radio, television, microwave, and various other man-made and naturally radiated emissions that fill the air. Sound waves can pass through solid walls, but light can't. X-rays can pass through soft human tissue, but not lead. Radio waves can pass easily through the air unless they encounter strong electromagnetic fields. And so on. Each energy form has its own family of characteristics and limitations, all functioning within what we easily accept as an integrated system, the cosmos. Similarly, all the planes of Earth act within a unified, integrated system, yet each has its own family of characteristics and limitations. It just happens that our corporeal awareness is so fixed on the characteristics of our atomical plane that we don't easily perceive the characteristics of other planes all about us. That, however, is the product of our human family of characteristics.

The structure of planes is one of a broken or divided continuum. Within the planet Earth, there is a set of planes that functions according to a framework of planetary integrity. Similarly, there are sets of planes associated with most atomical bodies within the cosmos. Each set of planes is a product of the local forces of the host entity, be it a planet, comet or single atom of hydrogen floating through space. Naturally, a planet such as ours offers far greater evolutionary potential than a single hydrogen atom, but the basic potential of physical behavior is much the same in both simple and complex systems. The more complex system merely represents a greater exploitation of potential than the simple system. Thus, our planet has some 21 planes whereas a single hydrogen atom floating through space may have only two or three secondary planes.

Because of this common range of behavior, our planet is as effective an illustration of the principles of inter-plane behavior as any other cosmic entity. Just as one atom can be expected to behave similarly here or in a galaxy light-years away, the interactive principles of the multi-plane system can be expected to behave much the same here as anywhere. Our planet, then, is a system of planes, each plane having a certain coherence of being within an overall context. This context is provided by a spectrum of energies. All the activity on our atomical plane and on every other potential plane of planet Earth is the result of this energy spectrum.

This energy spectrum has natural divisions based on its composite forces. Just as the material energies of our world take unique form within a unified context, the planes occupy specific portions of this larger energy spectrum. The physical framework of planes, then, is based on interlocking energy systems, all forged from a common spectrum. The energy systems themselves have internal properties and self-definition. All these energies relate to what we can call material reality; this spectrum of energies is appropriately termed the "material spectrum". This means its energies are material energies. Whereas our familiar spacetime system has its principle material manifestations in the form of atomical energies, the other planes have their own material manifestations. In all cases, however, the energies of the secondary planes and the atomical plane are closely intertwined and closely related. They form pockets of self within the material spectrum as a whole.

In this context, I am using the term "material" in a very specific way. Often in everyday speech we use the terms "material" and "physical" interchangeably. Strictly speaking, however, the term "material" refers to anything with a material nature, whereas the term "physical" refers to anything that physically operates. The terms may still seem synonymous, but consider once again that just as the terms "cosmos" and "universe" are not strictly synonymous, neither are "material" and "physical". Material nature is just a subset of physical nature. As I shall explain in the next few chapters, the universe extends well beyond our atomical cosmos, and even well beyond material nature.

Material nature forms a specific class or family of energies. These energies exist on a spectrum of physical behavior, much as the energies of our known world exist on spectrums. In fact, the energies of our world are just a part of the overall material spectrum. The planes occupy specific portions of the material spectrum, much as the bands of colors occupy specific portions of the light spectrum. Light, in fact, is just one tiny portion of the material spectrum. And just as light can be viewed as a series of colors or in unified terms as white light, we can view the material spectrum as a series of divisible planes or as a unified entity. Because I am attempting to classify aspects of our extended reality, I am speaking in this book in terms of a series of planes. This is because human consciousness is organized in such a way as to prefer viewing the environment in segmented terms. If, however, our minds were organized to perceive nature in holistic terms, it would be equally valid to describe Earth as an undivided field. In fact, the entire universe can be viewed as an undivided field. Our interest in classifying our environment stems from characteristics of our consciousness. This is a natural trait, but one that does enforce somewhat arbitrary views of nature. Keeping this in mind, we can consider that any enumeration of planes such as I am presenting in this book is just *one* means of presenting truth. Other divisions (and there are many metaphysical works that count different numbers of planes) may well be equally valid, *in their own terms*.

To use the energies of terrestrial earth as a further example, consider the somewhat arbitrary fashion with which we assign names to portions of the frequency spectrum. Light, radio, X-rays, sound, microwaves, and so on are all measurable divisions of the frequency spectrum, or bands. These bands are divided according to properties they have in terms of human perception and human-constructed measurement tools. The names of the bands are assigned to certain portions of an otherwise unbroken spectrum on the basis of certain properties, such as visibility. If we can see a portion of the spectrum, we call it visible light. If it is red, blue or yellow, we consider it a primary color of light, a subdivision of the visible light spectrum. Yet each color blends into the next, providing all the hues of the rainbow.

At either end of the light spectrum there is invisible light, then eventually other bands. Measured in Hertz (cycles per second), the various bands fill an unbroken continuum of the frequency spectrum. Light, for instance, operates at a much higher frequency than, say, sound, but both are a part of the same spectrum. Though there is a great physical difference in the method by which we perceive light and sound, both belong to a common spectrum. Similarly, all matter exists on a spectrum, of which the frequency spectrum as we know it is just one manifestation. The material spectrum extends beyond the range of atomical energies to other planes. To a degree, even the separation of planes is somewhat arbitrary, based on how living entities perceive breaks or divisions in the spectrum.

The actual divisions between the planes are real enough. They are formed by juxtapositions of energy that allow natural realms of effect. However, not all energies are inhibited by the separators, or restricted to acting within a particular plane. Certain energies can cross certain barriers, and other energies can't; in fact, what is a barrier to one may not be perceptible to another. Atomical energy, for example, cannot exceed the speed of light without internal transformation. If this happens, it ceases to be atomical energy and becomes something different. Conversely, other forms of energy can indeed supersede this barrier and effectively travel faster than the speed of light. Consciousness is an effect of such an energy. Thought does travel faster than the speed of light, but we have no device that can measure this effect other than our consciousness itself. Similarly, the soul crosses the barrier between the atomical plane and the Afterlife at death. This is a natural effect of separation from the flesh, an energy body physically joined with atomical energies of the biological body suddenly slipping out of the flesh to a different physical plane.

The potential range of behavior is very great within any plane, and coupled together, the planes create a vast realm of effect. The planes are like the layers of an onion, one laid over another. The layers touch, are part of a whole, but still provide unique spheres of activity for specialized material forms. Entities such as atoms are immutably tied to their home plane because it is their plane that gives them form. If an atom was to change its internal composition, then its constituent energies could indeed be transposed to another plane. This, in effect, is part of the function of the corporeal organism and the Spirit. One ingests food, the other transforms certain energies derived from that food into a new configuation that can be transported through the barriers between this world and others.

The barriers or divisions between planes, then, are not fixed. They are very real, but affect certain organizations of matter more than others. The actual energies that can pass any particular barrier depend on the composition of both the energy and the barrier. If "sympathetic" in their organization, one can pass through the other. If not sympathetic, the passage is blocked. This is much like the mutual repulsion of similar magnetic poles. Positive repels positive, negative repels negative, but turn either magnet around and the two leap together with startling rapidity. Negative and positive, in these terms, can be said to be sympathetic.

The interactions between any two planes depend on their relative state on the matter-energy spectrum. The matter spectrum is divided largely according to density of energy particles. Here, density has much the same connotation as it does the way we use it on our plane. Density is a characteristic of energy wave patterns forming themselves into units of measurable effect. One energy particle can slide between two other widely spaced particles, and not interact greatly with either. Such is the nature of the planes of Earth. Each plane slides between the others, causing scarcely a ripple between them. Effects are based on compatibility as much as proximity. In fact, proximity is a term that is only valid when we view the arrangement of matter from our spatial perspective.

At the base of this scale of matter density is the atomical plane. It is the most densely configured of all the planes, with the possible exception of such entities as neutron stars and black holes. These, however, are actually just extremely compacted atomical bodies and therefore rightly considered a part of our plane. The secondary planes take advantage of the remarkably focused concentrations of energy that form our plane to anchor their own existence. Although we do not perceive these interactions, terrestrial earth as an atomical body is actually holding the other planes of Earth in place. As well as providing a source of raw materials for their continued evolution, the terrestrial plane provides a focus of context. The other planes can act independently as organized entities only because the cosmic explosion of the Big Bang set the stage for the evolution of exactly this kind of material organization.

Although the other planes are less dense in matter structure, they are no less substantial. The discarnate soul's environment in the Afterlife, for example, seems just as solid to it as ours does to us. Solidity, like the subjective perception of light, is a product of the entity's consciousness as much as the external stimulus. We perceive a certain waveform or collection of waveforms as light, when in fact the perception of the quality light is actually occurring mostly within the brain and upper conscious. Atoms, which seem so solid when configured into something like a table or a chair, are really just patterns of particles and forces that on close examination have no true solidity at all. Matter takes its substance from tiny waveforms that have many interactions and physical characteristics, but none of which is solidity. Solidity is just another interpretation placed on our environment by our human perceptions and consciousness.

Life itself is just a set of waveforms, albeit a very complex one. In fact, life occupies a portion of the material spectrum, and does so in such a way that it can interact with many different planes. Each of the 21 planes of Earth supports its own range of lifeforms, the lifeforms themselves not just part of their worlds, but an integral factor in creating new worlds and new forms of material energy.

All these many energy forms can coexist because of natural variations. Each acts within its own context and only interacts directly with energies that are most similar or compatible. The properties of life, for example, are not greatly disturbed by electromagnetic fields. Life-energy is not directly affected in any significant way by gravity. This means the soul, in a sense, can fly. Yet where it flies is another issue. As long as it is anchored to a corporeal organism that does not fly, the soul does not fly either. Each form of energy has its own properties and fields. It acts along a certain portion of the material spectrum. There are natural divisions on this spectrum, and some divisions are enforced by other phenomena. Just think of the human being as a receptor that perceives only certain signals. Like a television tuned to receive UHF (ultra-high frequencies) or an AM/FM radio, the human life force has a certain range of frequencies. These frequencies are of an extraordinarily high nature in comparison with any technology we are familiar with in our world. However, they are based in a common system, the extended system of material energies of which this base plane is just a part.

Each plane is woven about the others, each differing in physical properties sufficiently so that its density of structure is never precisely matched by another. Thus, the planes coexist with little mutual interference, though there are always incidental crossovers. Lifeforms, because of their variable natures, are able to move from one physical realm of effect—one plane—to another. A discarnate soul, though normally not interacting directly with our terrestrial system, can indeed materialize briefly in our world under specific physical circumstances. This is a form of crossover, and such crossovers are the subject of more than one campfire tale.

Planes, in a way, behave on a physical level in much the same way man has tried to engineer the various frequency bands used for broadcasting. A certain amount of bandwidth is set aside for each channel. Regulatory agencies attempt to keep enough bandwidth between channels so they won't interfere with each other, but on a clear night signals in populated areas often get hopelessly tangled. Atmospheric skips and other natural phenomena cause further deviation from the intended pattern. Likewise, certain phenomena cause interference between planes. When that happens, a lifeform from another plane may appear in our world as an apparition. This is rare, but happens often enough for a mystique to evolve around such events. Although normally we perceive just one plane at a time, as a properly tuned radio perceives just one channel at a time, it is possible to perceive what we might term an inter-plane skip.

In many ways, human beings are like a radio receiver. Matter is organized in a particular way to relate to a certain range, the principles within that range depending on energy structure, base elements, and other characteristics. The barriers between planes are naturally occurring elements of physical relationships which serve to hold the planes apart. There may be interference, crossover or temporary blockages, but the overall effect is usually consistent. What belongs in one world normally stays there.

Not everyone who "sees" things is necessarily glimpsing life from another plane. On the other hand, religious experiences undoubtedly include many valid instances of true crossovers. When the devout see Jesus or the Virgin Mary on a hillside, it is difficult to ascertain whether they are truly experiencing some form of inter-plane effect or just conjuring an image through internal mental processes. The two events, as we shall see, are not so different. All our visual perceptions are produced by the brain's neurological responses to stimuli. It is just difficult at times to pinpoint the origins of the stimuli. Still, crossovers do occur, and much of man's mystical experience has been aimed at eliciting and controlling such phenomena. Astral projection is an instance of our life-energy passing into other planes while still maintaining a lifeline to the biological organism. The most common form of inter-plane crossover in our experience, however, is communication with discarnate souls and our guides.

This communication is possible because of the nature of the life-energies comprising living beings in our plane and others. Although the primary matter of our world—atomical particles—cannot cross into other planes, life-energies can. Furthermore, fields associated with those energies even more readily pass between worlds. Souls communicate easily with similar souls, wherever those souls happen to be. Our guides, so similar to us in soul-nature, are able to communicate with us on the level of the base soul. Our weakness is in terms of communicating with them in the higher levels of mental consciousness. To date, our most successful methods of doing so are through prayer, meditation, and mediumistic communications.

For the most part, the relationships between lifeforms on our plane and the others are oblique. The lifeforms of other planes are often as unaware of us as we are of them. However, there are special cases. The Guides of Man belong to a race of souls closely related to our soul-race. They and other races interact with us quite often and quite deliberately. We can perceive their communications because our life-energies are essentially compatible. We are close enough to each other on the life-energy spectrum that direct communications are relatively easy.

Direct communication in this sense involves a direct reception of thought-waves. This may involve direct stimulation of the nerve receptors of the brain by an external entity or via one of the lower levels of consciousness. This means another lifeform can directly stimulate your brain much as you do when you think. Instead of your own mind telling your body what to do, some external entity tells your body what to do. If this sounds to you like a monumental invasion of privacy, you're right. Direct stimulation of someone else's nervous system is normally not done lightly, although many principles of sorcery and witchcraft are based on exactly such a thing. Perhaps that is how the black arts earned such a shaded reputation.

However, external communication—and even direct stimulation of your nervous system—can be very beneficial. It can be the stimulus you need to throw yourself out of the way of an oncoming car. Stimulation of your thought patterns may give you the insight you need to solve a problem you have been struggling with. Also, there are the many forms of mediumship. Automatic writing, voice projection (this is when a discarnate speaks through a medium), and mental telepathy are forms of extraterrestrial communications. These communications, much like a telephone call from mother, are normally part of a natural guiding process that occurs to all of us on an ongoing basis whether we are intellectually aware of them or not.

Sometimes communications between planes are accidental. Under certain circumstances we perceive things not of this world because of natural phenomena that temporarily forge a link between planes. This may establish a communications channel from a soul that is not normally in contact with you, or you may just "tune in" to something that is happening elsewhere. Likewise, we send out all kinds of signals that can be perceived by any compatible entity that cares to pay attention. This type of thing is normally ignored by entities that can perceive it; it is viewed as a sort of "white noise" on the inter-plane channels of communication. There are even cases in which we can see an entity from another plane as it deliberately manifests itself in our world. This is another type of apparition, equally valid—if not more so—than the accidental variety. Similarly, we can also "material-ize" on other planes at will under certain conditions (though not, or course, in terms of moving the atoms of our bodies there). When this happens, it can be as surprising for whoever is on the other side as it is when *we* see an apparition.

We seldom allow ourselves to experience contact with other planes when in the waking state. Usually the systematic contact with our guides occurs on the deepest levels of consciousness. If it surfaces at all, it does so through dreams, impulses, and spontaneous thoughts we accept as our own. Not all of these restrictions are imposed by our intellectual orientation. A significant portion of the modern way of life involves shunning mystic arts such as mediumship. This has a definite blocking effect on nonterrestrial communications, as well as our interpretations thereof. However, the human corporeal organism is also an inhibiting factor.

Our bodies are evolved and equipped to deal with the realities of this world. Though contact with other planes can occur on a sensory level, this is normally quite limited. These natural limitations are enhanced by an intellectual orientation that resists acknowledging our spiritual talents. In spite of a growing awareness that psychic talents are very much a part of the natural order, people are still not comfortable with extrasensory perceptions. The cutting edge of sci-ence has its dull back; an area that isn't easily understood or explored through empirical means is all too often dismissed as irrelevant.

As well, the corporeal organism is biased in favor of the organic senses. Like a radio tuned to a single channel, we "tune out" what we would otherwise find disagreeable or even dangerously distracting. But if we try, we can usually succeed to some degree in stimulating our extrasensory abilities. Telepathy is one of the easiest of the ESP phenomena to test. We can send thoughts outward by deliberately attempting to do so; in fact, we broadcast all kinds of thoughts all the time. Often, these thoughts are acted upon by people we know, usually without their realizing their own thoughts had an external stimulus. Have you ever thought of someone and received a phone call from that person at that very moment? You can call it coincidence, but what really happens is that you receive the other person's thought as he is about to call you, or he responds to *your* thought of him. Either way, the impulse is often strong enough to motivate action. Such an impulse can carry across thousands of miles as easily as across town. Here, it is definitely our intellectual orientation that blocks our recognizing this very common phenomenon as a telepathic event. It is only one of the events that have caused "coincidence" to become a very overworked word in our lexicon.

In spite of the very real use of telepathy and other psychic abilities as part of the sorcerer's bag of tricks, we are not totally at the mercy of other people's thoughts. In fact, modern society has found an excellent defense against sorcery. There is a simple physical blocking effect in the psyche that functions according to depth of belief; the less we believe it is possible to receive telepathic thoughts, the harder it is to do so. Thus, modern man, by failing to believe in sorcery, has evolved a highly effective defense against it. This is a simplification, but highly accurate nonetheless. It is similar with other mystic techniques. If you do not clear a channel through a certain depth of belief, your efforts to use your psychic abilities will probably not be very successful. Somewhat frustratingly for psychical researchers, psychic abilities function best when left to their own intuitive devices. Nonetheless, the abilities can be controlled. With training, quite spectacular results can be achieved.

To develop psychic skills, a rigorous training process is required. Such training is at the heart of most mystic ritual. Ritual is an effective means of training the corporeal organism to admit experiences that can easily be ignored. In other words, you can train yourself to be more sensitive to what happens around you, including what happens on other physical planes. The yogi does this through meditation and discipline of the body and mind. So does the Karate master through Kime. These are techniques that grew out of young civilizations just a step away from their primitive roots. The people who developed the techniques recognized and perceived aspects of nature as their primitive forefathers did; their advance was to harness and enhance the abilities through training. The advent of civilization enabled a priest class to evolve that could devote itself to such studies. Ritual, though it has many manifestations, is important more as a tool by which the mind is concentrated than a set of step-by-step practices.

For modern man to rediscover his psychic skills, he must strip away the mental inhibitions imposed by modern thought processes. We have abilities we ignore, while at the same time we yearn to know what these abilities could easily reveal. A revived sense of mysticism and ritual in the modern world could put us in touch on a mental level with other worlds. To do so, however, would require rediscovery of ritualized training procedures that would strip away many of our current mental inhibitions, peel back our protective mechanisms, and expose our consciousness to many unpleasant truths about ourselves and our neighbors. This is essentially the reason telepathy and other extrasensory abilities are not well used: even if we generally believed such things to be possible, do we really want to expose our minds that fully to others?

In spite of our curious need to identify solely with our atomical existence and to shut out most of the nonatomical worlds around us, we do continue to have an awareness of other worlds. Folklore concerning the multi-plane structure of Earth is still strong, even in industrialized societies. Our physiological structure allows us to perceive things quite beyond the atomical. When this happens, a new campfire tale is born. If you scratch the surface a bit in any gathering of people, you will find that most people have a tale or two to tell about the unusual and unexplainable.

There is a high degree of prejudice against the paranormal in our culture. However, we must remember that so many strange things have been proved true that we should be as suspicious of our own motives as we are of new ideas or experiences. Though there are many frauds in the world who seek to benefit from the superstitions of others, there are far more people who bravely report the unexplained at the risk of public ridicule.

Take for instance the fact that polls have shown that most North Americans accept the existence of UFOs. Although science still officially reserves judgment, people reason that we have developed space travel, so why couldn't someone else? Rashes of sightings through the centuries have kept the idea from dying. Though I haven't personally seen an alien spacecraft, I have seen some Polaroid snapshots taken in northern Alberta by an oil rig worker. I was working as a photographer at the time and familiar with darkroom techniques. I can't think of any way those photographs could have been faked; they certainly weren't pictures of tinfoil plates on a string. Aside from publicity, which could be as negative for him as positive, what did the worker have to gain by approaching a reporter in his old home town? The fact is, he saw something definitely from out of this world, and was highly motivated in spite of potential ridicule to share it with his peers.

There comes a point when refusing to believe something is counterproductive, even if evidence is not ironclad in scientific terms. People hold their beliefs because of what they are taught, what they experience, and what they intuitively reason can be real. Often, people have new experiences which force them to revisit what they have been taught. Though there is no concrete proof that UFOs exist, or that the soul survives bodily death, or that there are other planes, there is much circumstantial evidence and much intuitive reason to believe that these things are true. The fact that life leaves a body does not empirically mean life has ceased. It is equally valid to suppose it has only changed state. And that, in fact, is really what happens.

This change of state is called crossing over. Souls cross over from this plane to the Afterlife. From there, the view of nature is much less inhibited. From there, other planes are more obvious to the unbridled perceptions of the naked soul. And from there, contact with living entities on other planes is more open, less dependent on fortune and chance, and definitely sought out and encouraged by most actively evolving souls.

To understand our place in the universe, we need to understand that the universe is not just multi-dimensional, but that it has infinite dimensions. Within the universe, each aspect of nature has its own functional organization. In some cases this organization allows the unit to appear to be independent. This is certainly the case with our cosmos, at least from our in-flesh perspective. However, this perspective changes when the soul separates from the flesh. The new perspective— and the new reality of the Afterlife—has a significant impact on its view of nature. The planes of Earth, though they have an apparent independence, are actually a part of an integrated planet, which in turn is integrated with the entire universe.

The specific characteristics of each lifeform are tailored through evolution to suit its particular niche. In human terms, our niche encompasses two worlds, the corporeal reality of terrestrial earth and the discarnate existence of the Afterlife. One world provides raw material energies and experience; the other provides a place to consolidate these energies and experiences, and plan for future growth. These two worlds provide us with a means of regeneration and growth. They allow us to evolve into greater entities. At some point, we will evolve to the point where we will as souls join a higher plane to continue our material evolution. In the meantime, we are well suited to our niche. Other lifeforms, we will someday acknowledge, are equally suited to their own niches in their own planes, even if we can't see them.

Chapter Nine
THE LEVELS OF UNIVERSE

The universe in its most elemental form is a single field. Everything that exists, no matter how complex, is a convolution or expression of the universal force. We derive our understanding of the universe from an understanding of its parts.

But to divide the universe into parts is a conceptual exercise that has an inherent flaw. You cannot truly break anything out of the universe and call it a "part" because there is no certain way of determining when something stops being itself and begins being something else. For example, there is no line between your self and your external environment. You are defined in relation to everything external to you, and you influence everything around you. Any aspect of the universe has a primary focus or realm of effect. Each and every aspect of the universe interacts with the universe as a whole. In its broadest possible context, each and every aspect of the universe *is* the entire universe.

However, it remains useful to divide the universe into parts for component studies. We systematically analyze and classify our selves and our environment, setting out the building blocks of nature in terms we perceive and understand. Each discipline of science, for instance, selects some aspect of nature for intensified study. However, though the specialist may work within a very narrow focus, his success depends on how well his ideas mesh with the total scientific paradigm. Although he may immerse himself in his special realm of interest, he must never forget that it is part of a unified whole, the entire universe. As a disgruntled physics student once quipped, "No sooner do you try to isolate something than you find it is attached to everything else in the universe".

Even with its problems, compartmentalizing nature is a valid pursuit. There is an apparent organization to the universe. In general, we share a common perception of this organization. Presumably, what we view as an identifiable part of our environment (say a tree or a river) has some justifiable basis for being viewed in those terms. In other words, we must assume the item has some special characteristics that enable us to distinguish it as a unique entity within its complete context. We don't perceive our environment as an amorphous blob; rather, we distinguish many classes and organizations of physical reality. Our intellectual exercises, then, are geared to devising intelligent and practical models of our environment that offer the most effective compartmentalization.

Dividing nature into parts helps us explain what is happening around us. We don't require explicit understanding of every aspect of every part to make general statements concerning nature. A look at the sky reveals the sun, clouds, birds. Each of these observations is based on a classification of reality. We instinctively separate parts from the whole so that we may identify potential actions of our own. Our perceptions are not complete, but sufficient to determine potential effects from a set of conditions. If, for example, a bird of prey swoops toward our small pet dog, our reactions are quite different than if we merely observe a scudding cloud. We needn't know the bird's entire evolutionary history or life-patterns to realize there is potential danger. Likewise, we needn't know all about meteorology to recognize a cloud.

This instinctive compartmentalization is reinforced at every level of our being. We need it to survive as biological organisms; we also need it to grow and evolve as souls. The evolution and well being of the soul depend on its coherent assessment and evaluation of its environment just as biological survival depends on instinct and rational decision-making. Even the simplest lifeforms distinguish between aspects of their environment; life depends on it. The only true differences between lifeforms are in the manner and degree with which they pursue their respective analysis of their environments. The one-celled microorganism in a drop of water on a microscope slide that swims away from a light is behaving very similarly in primary motivation as a person who dodges a careless motorist. Both are responding to a stimulus in their environment.

Our intellectual pursuits through science are only one expression of a very primal urge to differentiate between aspects of our environment. Our focus on the atomical plane during corporeal incarnations is the result of a long biological history that led us to highlight certain perceptions and block out others. The bottom line is that the base soul acts from a broader perspective than the surface mind. The discarnate consciousness is able to view the universe in expanded terms, resulting in the discarnate entity usually holding a wider framework or paradigm of nature. The soul accepts the paradigm implicitly, just as biological organisms implicitly accept the environment most obvious to them. My goal in this chapter is to outline some implicit perceptions that have resulted in what may be termed the soul's paradigm of universal organization. This is not a definitive theory, but merely one that expresses a way in which differentiation can occur within the unified framework of the universe without imposing strict limits on the total potential creativity of the universe. In effect, it is a means by which the infinite whole can be contemplated in terms of an infinite number of finite parts.

The soul's paradigm involves a fundamental architecture my guides describe as the "levels of universe". This term is offered as much to satisfy the purposes of language and communications as to define physical divisions of nature. However, the universe does lend itself to such divisions, if only in very general terms. This paradigm is based on two essential assumptions: one, that all of nature is unified and must therefore be unified by some lowest common denominator, something we can call the universal force; and two, that because nature is highly organized, this organization must be based on progressively higher orders of organization of the universal force. The universe is composed of infinite levels or functional units, each of which is intrinsically different from all the others.

Though simple, this paradigm provides a flexible framework that can be used to study and analyze the universe regardless of how vast or complex it actually is. It allows elements of nature to be cataloged as discovered, without disrupting the overall model. The key element is the level or basic building block of the universe. This model or division of the universe is not meant to suggest some immutable or frozen blocks of reality, but a way of systematically resolving major categories of universal events in terms our science-driven cultures can appreciate. Remember, our cultures have presented us with a unique way of thinking. We have to be aware that it not only provides a framework we can use to view nature, but also enforces inevitable limitations. In other words, even as science systematically catalogs and classifies this world and thereby achieves a greater understanding of nature, this very classification enforces rather arbitrary divisions between otherwise inseparable events.

The universal force, as the fundamental essence of nature, is manifested in its most elemental state of organization as universal energy. Universal energy is really just an inflection of the term universal force, or an expression of the unification of energy and force at the most elementary level. Force is a product of nature that implies an active process or conveys a field; energy implies a condition or arrangement of nature, a result of a force or forces. At its most elemental state of being, the universal force creates universal energy, which is then configured into higher states of force and energy.

The elemental state of universal energy, what we might call the first order of organization, can obviously be subjected to further organization. We know this because we perceive higher forms of organization within our environment, such as our own selves. If we accept the twin assumptions that there is at once a simplest form of organization and highly complex forms of organization, we must also accept that there are many steps in between, including a second order of organization, a third, a fourth, and so on. A level of universe is a label we can affix to a primary differentiation within the universal energy. This is the point at which multiple entities take form within nature, the first step in the formation of higher orders of organization.

A level of universe, then, is not just a simple layer of physical reality, but a specific class of physical existence arising out of the universal field. It is a primary subdivision of nature, an area in which a set of laws and properties exist that give it some essential unity of action. It establishes a potential range of behavior, based on that first step of differentiation within an otherwise homogeneous whole. Although it interacts with all other levels of universe, it primarily focuses its activity within itself. It acts virtually as a universe unto itself, just as the various planes of Earth act virtually as worlds unto themselves. At the same time, you might say they act within each other, their interactions controlled by their internal characteristics.

The infinity of the universe is achieved by the fact that there is an infinite number of levels of universe (and infinite "potential" levels, or levels that do not yet exist). Such infinity is possible because there is no limit to the ways the universal energy can manifest itself in higher forms of organization. Each primary field established within the universal context is essentially one aspect of the universe breaking itself off into a finite sort of existence. It will have limits to its duration and self, just as any part of the universe does. Defining a part within the whole inherently means assigning limits to that part. At the same time, the infinite primary building blocks, though they are finite entities in and of themselves, also have infinite potential creativity for further differentiation and organization within themselves.

The best analogy for the concept of the universal level is the numerical scale. Each whole number is analogous to one universal level. It is a fragment of an infinite series of whole numbers, each number having an inherent definition of self and its own unique properties. Each number is finite, yet has a potentially infinite internal creativity in that it can be divided into any number or kind of fractions. You can have thirds, halves, or any type of fraction; you can view part of a whole number or all of it, depending on your choice or purpose. Similarly, each level of universe has an inherent self, but can be viewed or organized in any number of ways. At all times, however, the levels of universe must respect universal laws and interactions between levels, just as numbers and fractions must always obey mathematical laws.

The unity of each universal level establishes a base of activity for a certain portion of the universal field. This sets the stage for very specific types of behavior within any particular universal level. The universal level has as its lowest common denominator a base energy. This base energy is a single permutation or arrangement of the universal energy. This first step of higher organization sets the stage for the types of further organization that can occur within the specific field of that level of universe. Higher orders of organization then evolve through subsequent permutations of the energy trapped or engaged within that level of universe. It then becomes a field of activity unto itself, one level among all other levels that evolved from their own unique derivation of the universal energy. All subsequent orders of organization or differentiation within the level of universe are based on the specific properties made possible by the very first level of differentiation. It is like a journey that begins with a single step, all steps leading in the direction set by the first.

In these terms, then, we are a product of a single level of universe in all the infinite numbers of levels, just as we are part of a single galaxy in all the galaxies of the cosmos. Whatever we are, we have evolved through the progressive steps of evolving order within our specific level of universe. If we had the technology or mathematical models, we could trace the physical evolution of each particle of energy or matter of our selves to their source in a particular permutation of the universal energy. Similarly, we can trace the relationships between any type of matter in all of our universal level to that single source. If we belonged to some other level, we could do the same, only we would be tracing an entirely different set of forces and physical patterns. It just happens that in our level of universe, the base substance or energy is matter energy; all that we know, both in terms of our corporeal selves and in terms of the soul, exists as the result of forces related to matter energy.

Our level of universe is the field in which all potential matter energies can exist; matter is the primary manifestation of our level of universe. Souls therefore call it the Material Level. It interacts with all other levels, as all other levels interact with each other. Yet its primary laws of internal organization are those related to matter. Matter here is defined as all matter energies, not just those of our atomical environment. This means all the potential planes that can be created based on the material spectrum of energy discussed in the previous chapter are a part of the Material Level. The unified field of all the planes of Earth, for example, is an indication of the potential range of creativity within the Material Level. Just as the internal make-up of this level is that of matter, each of the other levels of universe has its own internal make-up. It is one off-shoot of the universal energy, among an infinity of potential off-shoots, all of which exist in each its own unique terms.

Each level of universe that exists is juxtaposed against all the others in the curiously parallel manner the universal force allows. Each evolves in its own way, for the most part acting independently of all the others. Once energy is configured within one level of universe, it is committed to deriving its further organization from the properties dominant within that level. This means that as part of one universal level, we cannot ever become a part of another, at least not as highly organized entities. Though a soul can travel from plane to plane within the Material Level, it cannot travel between levels of universe. Energy can only be transferred between levels if reduced to the simplest form possible—the universal energy—then reorganized to fit the pattern inherent in another existing level or a new pattern altogether to begin yet another off-shoot from the root of universal existence.

Once a universal level is established, it has an inherent unity. Although it is by no means permanent or immutable, it has a certain stability of self within the framework of nature. It can be studied, analyzed, and explored. Nature reconfigures itself constantly, and universal levels come and go. But usually they have a very great durability. I am struggling here not to say that they endure for a long time, because time is a property inherent to only one plane within our single level of universe. It is doubtful whether any other level of universe has planes, let alone time. The levels of universe are that alien from one another.

To some degree, my use of the term "level of universe" is arbitrary. I could just as well say "mega-aspect of universe" or some other term that conveys the meaning of a major portion of existence. My intent in using this specific term, though, is that it conveys a precise connotation of divisibility. I am not intending to convey an image of layers in the progressive sense, as in the geological layers of earth. The levels of universe are simultaneous events and mutually exclusive. The word "level" indicates something that can be divided in some way into measurable portions. This concept shows us that not only is there a much greater framework to think of in terms of interacting worlds, such as the planes of Earth (which is boggling enough in itself), but that the organization of the universe does not stop there. It continues in infinite directions, in ways our imaginations cannot possibly comprehend. I must satisfy myself with such weak words as "alien" and "differentiation"—Jung would say "individuation"—when talking about things of a magnitude that no words truly convey.

The levels of universe do not just end and become something else completely. There is a transition between them. Levels are more similar to some than others, and some interact more closely than others. Just as we can classify animals into various orders, families, and species, we can classify the levels of universe. At a base level of consciousness we can recognize certain interactions between our level and others; on that basis we can know there is more to the universe than even the multi-plane system of Earth. Still, a soul cannot go and explore another universal level any more than the atoms of our corporeal bodies can be transported to the Afterlife.

In each and every model of each and every aspect of the universe, the classification of parts and subparts is determined to a large degree by divisions inherent in nature. The limits of one part or subpart may not be precise, but there are indeed natural divisions between aspects of an ultimately unified whole. In our cosmos, there may be no clear division between one galaxy and another or between one star system and another, but it is certain that the concepts of galaxies and star systems are valid. We can debate where to draw the dividing line, but we must all agree that one system ends and another begins. It is thus with every subdivision within nature, including the levels of universe.

The base soul meets the challenge of discovering what lies beyond this universal level in much the same way as modern scientists study subatomic particles. In physics, interactions between known particles are carefully observed to gather clues to other potential particles. Then the known base of data, though incomplete, is used to construct a theory that accounts for as much as possible of what is known. The scientist can discover new things just by applying good logic and being sensitive to the symmetries of nature.

For instance, scientists have found a negative particle—or anti-particle—to be associated with most subatomic particles so far discovered. When a new particle is discovered, it now seems reasonable to expect to discover an associated anti-particle. By and large, this usually proves to be the case. The discovery of the anti-particle is made easier by the fact that the scientist knows what characteristics to expect based on his knowledge of the positive particle. He can then set up his experiments and equipment accordingly, increasing his chances of discovering the anti-particle. The base or discarnate soul applies similar principles in analyzing the interactions between our level and others. In fact, we can do the same at a mental level if we sensitize ourselves to the existence of parallel levels and planes and their interactive forces; the concept of antimatter itself is suggestive of a related level of universe, perhaps an antimatter level. If the universal energy can be distorted so that there is what we regard as a positive field, might there be a negative field as well to counterbalance it?

It is theoretically possible to identify each and every one of the infinite levels of universe based on the interactions between them. Practically, however, this is not even remotely feasible. No lifeform, I suspect, is sufficiently evolved to perceive more than a few closely related levels of universe. Still, the principle that there are infinite levels is accepted in soul-worlds because the principle of the infinite universe is accepted. It is not conceivable how the universe can have any true limits in the sense of having a beginning, end, or edges. Ergo, it must be infinite. There are limitations to aspects or parts of the universe, but the universe itself is infinite.

Modern science has yet to develop the concept of the universal level. Even if existing tools were adequate to detect interactions between our level and others, no scientist I'm aware of has yet framed the concept of multidimensional existence in these exact terms so that he would be able to test this theory. However, interactions between our level of universe and others can indeed be detected with atomical instruments, providing the instruments are calibrated to do so. We only need to know what to look for and how to develop the appropriate tools. It is a similar exercise to that of isolating antiparticles. The formation of a genuine scientific theory of parallel levels of universe, however, is some time away yet. Still, scientists do like to speculate about "parallel universes". There is no reason that these speculations cannot be fulfilled, though I prefer the term "level of universe". From our single vantage point (or, equally, any other vantage point in the universe), it is theoretically possible to unravel the entire universe, piece by piece, level by level. Because every aspect of the universe is linked to every other aspect by universal laws, these relationships are discoverable.

Even so, the most far-reaching attempts to explore other levels of universe, theoretically or otherwise, will ultimately be stymied by the alien natures of the different levels. There are physical limits for contact between one level and another. The very natures that give each its coherence and independence also cloister it to some degree from even the most closely related levels. By nature and definition any level of universe is vastly different than the most closely related levels. Even within a single level such as ours, we can see how the potential range of natural differentiation is astounding; we can see that from studying just our atomical plane—one portion of our level of universe.

My objective in presenting this theory is to reflect some of the potential diversity of the universe, even in these superficial terms. I want us to realize that not only is there more to reality than this atomical plane, but there is more than an entire set of planes. The Material Level is just one potential construct within the universal field; in spite of its incredible internal diversity, it is just one among an infinite number of equally expansive aspects of reality. The universe is vaster and more complex than any theory ever devised by man. If we wish to understand how physical reality functions, we must be aware of how extensive physical reality is.

We must continue to map the universe through systematic scientific investigation. We can do this, and perhaps even discover neighboring levels of universe, because of the unerring consistency of universal laws. Although our understanding of these laws will always be incomplete and imperfect, we can always improve our knowledge. We do not need to know every aspect of a law to understand how it is crucial to the physical configuration of nature. We may, for instance, speak of gravity as if it is a single thing. In fact, gravity is the expression of many orders of law, culminating in a set of effects we view as the force of gravity. We know that gravity is what makes a ball fall down after being thrown into the air; we also know that gravity keeps our planet from dashing away across space instead of steadily orbiting the sun. At the same time, we don't *really* know what gravity is. We don't know what causes it, what controls it, or how it came to be. It is a part of our environment that we have defined to some extent because some of its effects are obvious to us.

Consistency is the reason we call gravity a law. We know with absolute certainty that any ball thrown into the air will fall down unless someone or something catches it. There are other laws we know as well, still others that we struggle to define. All of them represent aspects of our environment, which we seek to understand in an orderly way. Our environment already has order in and of itself. Our goal as intelligent entities is to organize our understanding of our environment. We intuitively know how to interact with our environment, but intuition does not satisfy our reason. We want more than intuitive interaction. By seeking to understand the laws of the universe, we seek ways of controlling aspects of our environment to serve our own wants and needs.

This desire stems from a very deep psychical source, the base soul. The human soul desires to understand the universe, or at least what it perceives of the universe, in as fully rationalized a manner as possible. Souls study the universe continuously, in flesh and out. The flesh offers specific and unique opportunities for studying aspects of nature; so does the discarnate state. Each state presents its own unique perspective. The soul, with its insatiable desire to understand all it can, uses each phase of its incarnations as an opportunity for study.

The experiences we glean from this environment have very specific and indispensable uses for the soul. Although, for example, our sciences focus on the atomical plane, the soul has already rationalized in its own way the nature of atomical reality. The soul assimilates knowledge by direct contact with subject matter; it understands the workings of much of atomical nature by contact with a single atom. The understanding is intuitive, at a level we might describe as instinctual. Similarly, the soul can perceive interactions between planes and between levels of universe. The soul, through these remarkable powers of direct or holistic assimilation of knowledge, can achieve in a moment what all our sciences have taken centuries to achieve.

This information, unfortunately, is to a large degree shielded from the waking mind by the middle conscious. Still, each and every one of us intuitively understands the true nature of the universe. There is a repository of knowledge and experience in the base soul that isn't completely available to the waking consciousness. This is why we have scientists who research the nature of reality; this is why even primitives form mythologies about the formation and order of their environment. The very root of our consciousness drives us to make sense of our environment.

Science is not likely to discover any other levels of universe in our corporeal lifetimes. If we are lucky, we may witness the discovery of other planes of Earth. Even that, however, would be a giant step in scientific understanding of universal organization. There is purpose and design in every facet of nature, and the universal level is a useful concept for collecting our thoughts about infinity. It allows us to apportion an infinite whole into finite parts, just as we divide the numerical scale into whole numbers. And just as we have learned to accept that the numerical scale is infinite, we can learn that the universe is infinite. Though always dealing primarily with the immediate reality of terrestrial earth, we can at least be superficially aware that an infinity of existence lies before us, awaiting exploration.

Chapter 10
THE MATERIAL LEVEL

The Material Level is the product of matter energies, its base matter energy one elemental configuration of the universal force. As a field of action and reaction, the Material Level has a unity of self based on what sorts of activity are possible according to its internal laws and forces. It includes the atomical plane and all planes derived from the atomical plane, the planes being the principle manifestation of material nature. Other levels, of course, have their own particular manifestations in their own terms, each of them respectively forming their own field of action and reaction. Each level of universe is a sub-field of the overall universal field.

The qualities and characteristics of the Material Level are largely defined by its inhabitants. The nature of the universal force is such that any portion of the universe can be viewed in any number of ways. The view, of course, depends on the viewer. In our case, we have a particular human point of view as terrestrial lifeforms. At the same time, we have a particular point of view as soul-entities. Either way, we view the universe in terms of matter energies. Material nature is our most immediate level of physical reality and the only one apparent to us at present.

Matter energies form one class of physical reality, all manifestations of which can be traced to a single specialized differentiation within the universal energy, that is, the base matter energy. This basic manifestation of nature drives all further developments within the Material Level, including all aspects of our being as souls and corporeal entities.

It is quite important to understand how flexible the universal energy really is. It configures itself in infinite ways, with infinite inflections on any particular theme. Material nature is just one theme or set of rules that has come into existence. It just happens that this set of rules governs our existence, both as animals and soul-entities. We are indelibly a part of material nature, even though in the face of the entire universe, material nature is just a small sample of what is possible. It is one level among infinite levels.

At this point, I want to make it perfectly clear what I mean by "material nature". I do not intend for the term "material" to be synonymous with "atomical", nor with "physical". Each of these terms has its own specific meaning in the hierarchy of nature. "Physical" nature is anything that exists, that is, anything within the universe. "Material" nature is anything that is derived from one specific permutation—the base matter energy—of the physical energy of the universe. "Atomical", which is a term seldom used in English, as people usually substitute "material" or "physical" in its place, is anything directly relating to the atoms of our visible cosmos. Each subdivision of this hierarchy, then, progressively defines finer divisions of nature. Each term—physical, material and atomical—represents a progressively smaller subcategory of nature. As corporeal entities, we are atomical; our bodies are constructed of atoms. As soul-entities, however, we are constructed of a different category of material energies; the material energies of the soul are called soul-energy and life-energy.

This terminology is more precise than we are accustomed to using. We tend to be very imprecise in our world when we talk about material nature because we tend to separate "energy" from "matter". However, atomical matter as we know it is just one manifestation of the universal energy. It will become more and more important to remember this when science learns more about nonatomical systems. I believe much of our modern reluctance to accept such phenomena as precognition, telepathy, and the survival of the soul is the result of our indistinct notions of what does and does not constitute material nature. By habitually thinking of "atomical" nature as "material" nature, we have ended up creating such concepts as "supernatural" and "magic" for things that do not fit our normal terrestrial understanding.

A more useful framework is to think of nature in terms of "atomical" versus "nonatomical", "material" versus "nonmaterial", and so on, but never "physical" versus "nonphysical" or "supernatural". I don't believe there is anything that is nonphysical or supernatural. As far as I am concerned, if something exists, it is physical. If we do not understand how something can be physical, it is only because we haven't yet learned about the physical laws that govern its behavior. There is nothing that is beyond nature, nothing that is outside the universe. The universe is "All that Is".

Obviously, I am proposing that we redirect our thinking to some degree. If we wish to consider the reality of such things as ESP or divine providence, we must consider them as part of the universe. We may elect to define them as being beyond the atomical or even as being beyond the material, but we can never define them as being beyond the physical. If there is a God or a Creator then that entity, whatever it is, is also a part of the physical universe.

I am not just playing with semantics. Careful definition is the essence of human communications. Our minds require careful definition and classification of events and objects so that we can rationally assimilate an understanding of our environment. In other words, we are accustomed by long habit and evolution to assimilating knowledge in categorical terms. We mentally establish categories and fill them with units of interest. At more elemental levels of consciousness, such categorization is not necessary. The base soul, for example, is fully capable of perceiving and interacting with its environment in terms of direct, holistic perceptions. It does not require the imposition of dividing lines between aspects of nature that we do at a mental level. Thus, in pure terms, we do not need such concepts as levels of universe or individuality; all is one. This means our categorical view of reality is largely an artificial one. However, it also happens to be the way our minds work, and in that very valid sense, we have no choice other than to continue classifying each aspect of our environment.

The paradigm I am offering in this book is tailored to serve the needs of our current orientation of consciousness, that is, the waking self or what you would call "you". I hope to present a view of our physical universe that simultaneously reflects something of its infinity and its flexibility, while also accurately describing its highly ordered nature. There are indeed infinite levels of universe, categories of existence that have little direct effect on one another. These tremendous divisions of nature go their own way within the universal context, forging within themselves infinite varieties of highly ordered substances. Laws govern all the activity, though the laws themselves are just statements that reflect the activity.

Within our level of universe, the predominant manifestations of organization are the planes. Each plane is a distinct layer of physical nature, specifically a distinct layer of material nature. Our atomical cosmos is just one of those layers. My description of the planes—and more so the levels of universe—is very much colored by my own perceptions of nature. Any living consciousness can only interpret reality according to its own experience; I am no exception. The imperfection of my description is therefore the result of *my* imperfect perceptions of the universe. Like any other human being, I am forced to use terminology and analogies that grow out of a terrestrial experience, neither of which are capable of truly describing or relating to nonterrestrial events. Perhaps sadly, we must recognize that we cannot even describe terrestrial events as they really are.

The human mind, like any other device, does not perceive the complete reality of any event or object. In other words, we do not perceive reality as it really is. We only perceive portions of it, then interpret these portions in incomplete and at times inaccurate ways. Our mental abstractions are assimilations based on incomplete information, partially digested bits of information entering our minds in a somewhat haphazard fashion. We are devices that perceive portions of the environment, that achieve some rudimentary appreciation for these portions, then act on this appreciation in our own interest. If we are successful, we assume that our perceptions and interpretations must be in some way accurate, or if not accurate, at least useful. We have no way of knowing, however, how accurate any of our perceptions really are.

The accuracy of our perceptions is ultimately determined by how useful they are. We have augmented our native senses with tools and machinery that sometimes do a remarkable job in measuring events within our cosmos. Using massive particle accelerators, we can trace the path of tiny neutrinos, small, seemingly indivisible points of substance that hardly interact with other subatomic particles. It took years for physicists to be able to detect these tiny points of matter, all the while doubting whether they actually exist. Yet since then, their properties have been explored in some detail. At least one prominent physicist believes there may be so many neutrinos filling space that they may actually account for most of the matter in the cosmos. This is only one example of how the limits of human perception can be pushed outwards in pursuit of broader and more accurate paradigms of nature. And yet all this knowledge is based on fragmentary understandings, mere glimpses of truth.

Even more revealing is knowing that most of our knowledge is based on atomical science. We know very little about anything beyond atomical nature. The atomical cosmos has been the subject of study of all our physical sciences; only psychology and parapsychology have tried to reach beyond the atomical to study what may be nonatomical phenomena. Yet neither psychology nor parapsychology has any paradigm of nonatomical consciousness; both only treat events of consciousness, without any true understanding of the cause of those events. There is no science of the soul.

Such a science must be willing to explore beyond atomical phenomena in quest of explaining human experience. Human consciousness, although interactive with the corporeal organism, is separable from that organism. The soul survives bodily death. While in flesh, we experience many things that are nonatomical, but often fail to recognize them as such. Without a paradigm of nature that allows nonatomical events to coexist with atomical events, we wind up believing in the "supernatural" rather than the "nonatomical". Our sciences are so atomically oriented that there is virtually no objective way people can interpret human spiritual events. Science cannot currently explain precognition, the survival of the soul, reincarnation, or many other events of consciousness that apparently transcend the atomical organism. The individual's only recourse after experiencing such events is to ignore them or consider them in nonscientific terms. My goal in presenting my paradigm of universal organization is an attempt, however limited it may be, to provide some rudimentary paradigm for the thoughtful appraisal of a physical universe that includes all the nonatomical events of consciousness we have become familiar with. We have to be able to deal with such events rationally, though science to date has not even successfully explained thought.

Such a paradigm is the first step in dealing with disparate events that do not fit current physical theory. Although future work will expose its limitations, my paradigm offers an immediate framework for thoughtful analysis of any events we experience, whether familiar or unfamiliar. The framework allows the categorization of any type or range of experience in terms that do not require rejecting any existing physical theory. In other words, atomical theory is left to define atomical reality, but other theories must be devised to explain everything else. There is, therefore, no such thing as the supernatural or magic in the historical sense. There are only laws, known and unknown.

The laws we discover through our physical sciences are indeed uncovering the workings of the layer of reality most obvious to us. However, it is a mistake to interpret the atomical cosmos as being the total universe. The mistake is believing our perceptions are sufficient to view most of what exists. Instead, we should realize that our perceptions only enable us to view a smattering of what exists; indeed, only a smattering within one universal level.

The universal level is a concept that can be thrown out altogether once the premise of an infinite universe is fully accepted. However, it is useful as long as we use mental processes that require the division of reality into categories. If we are to understand in any way how a single, uniform substance can be convoluted into infinite varieties of more complex substances, we need to have some concept of progressive organization. From our point of view, it is contradictory to say that everything exists at once in every possible permutation. Yet in universal terms, this is exactly the case. The problem is not that such a thing is impossible, but that our minds are incapable of truly rationalizing and assimilating that unit of knowledge. We are bound by our own limitations of cognition.

Our limits of understanding are largely drawn by our limits of perception. If we accept that the universe is bounded by the edges of space, we have no choice other than to conceive of how every aspect of our experience originates within that framework. For atomical events, such a conception is easy. We have quite handily explained most macroscopic atomical phenomena and have also gotten quite sophisticated in our exploration of subatomic phenomena. However, certain events keep occurring that atomical theory does not explain. If we contend that the atomical cosmos is the entire universe, our only choices are to either reject unexplainable phenomena or hope they will someday be explained in atomical terms. But there is a third alternative. This is that reality may be far vaster than we perceive.

What we habitually overlook is that our perceptions are geared to a particular kind of reality. We perceive certain phenomena in certain ways. We do not perceive *all* phenomena in *all* ways, which is the only way we could ever truly claim to be on the verge of understanding all of the universe. Although we have learned a lot about atomical nature, we have barely scratched the surface of the universe.

As biological animals, humans have a definite focus on the atomical plane, a world of molecular structures and electromagnetic and gravitational fields. We are sustained by a physical plane that seems solid, durable and independent of our own conscious selves. This is a very formidable perception, and one so natural to us we seldom think of challenging it. However, this is exactly what we must do if we really want to observe the universe, and not just the atomical cosmos. Our perspective gives us an open window on a very thin slice or portion of nature. Although it may have been inevitable, our perspective has also inclined us to forget about aspects of nature we *can't* see.

Think for a moment about the nature of your perceptions. Note how you only perceive certain aspects of an object: you *see* a chair, but you don't hear it; you *hear* music, but you don't smell it. Imagine what it would be like if those perceptions were reversed, that you could actually hear the vibrations of the molecules comprising the chair or that you could smell the sound waves. Such a turnabout may seem utterly absurd at first glance, but really isn't. If your ear were sensitive enough, you could indeed hear vibrations of atoms in the chair. If your organic organization were different, you might indeed interpret sound as smell. It just happens that you use a particular set of abilities as you have come to know them. In each case, the true perception is the result of your organic chemistry. What you perceive as smell is something perceived through your nose; what you perceive as sound is perceived through your ears. Yet you can also feel vibrations with your skin receptors. You can allow sounds to evoke memories of certain smells. Your abilities are intertwined, each presenting to your mind a particular image or set of characteristics. Your mind then interprets them as it sees fit.

When we use our organic senses, we are inclined to make several assumptions. One is that the object of our perceptions is truly there; second, that its true self in some way resembles our perceptions; and third, that our perceptions are in some way indicative of the total reality of the object. And yet, in our heart of hearts, we know all three of these assumptions are false.

Even combining our senses does not tell us the full nature of any object. Each sense is aimed at a specific type of physical effect. The eyes detect light, the ear drum vibrates sympathetically with sound waves, and the nose detects tiny concentrations of molecules. In fact, our perceptions are based not on these precise physical events but on the interpretation of these events made by our brain and mind. We also rely on some perceptions more than others: sight is our primary tool of perception.

Each of our senses has a certain range of perception. Although the eye is delicately constructed to perceive light, it does not perceive ultraviolet light. And yet ultraviolet light has a direct effect on us; it can burn the skin. Our failure to see it does not mean it is not a light form, but simply that our eyes cannot see all forms of light. In fact, we can devise machines that detect ultraviolet light, the machines acting the role of an extended biological sense. All our machines serve a similar purpose; each is aimed at extending our abilities to perceive the environment.

Our perceptions, in other words, are not just the result of the environment, but also the individual. In the first place, we only perceive what we *can* perceive. In the second place, we perceive pretty much as we *want* to perceive. If we do not have organs and neurological pathways for the detection of certain events, we do not perceive them directly. If we are capable of detecting them, then we still have a certain amount of choice as to whether we will indeed perceive them. The mind has a very prominent role in our perceptions; we can decide to close our minds to pain and stick a pin through a thumb. The nervous system is driven not just by its environment, but by the individual. There are even a few rare individuals who have a dysfunction of the brain that blends their perceptions of events; when they hear music, a strong image of a marble archway may present itself to their mind, or they may see pink when they taste certain foods. This disorder is called synesthesia, or a joining of the senses.

Our nervous system is just one means of perceiving patterns within nature. Everything in nature is a pattern of some sort. We define patterns somewhat arbitrarily, based on the perceptions available to us. We see patterns in the physical make-up of our world and our selves. Without knowing otherwise, we are forced to assume that our perceptions convey some essence of truth. We never know how accurate the impressions in our minds really are, but we trust the consistency of our perceptions so that we may go about our daily lives. We have learned to trust our perceptions because we have needed to; we simply could not survive if we could not act on our perceptions.

Still, we should not confuse consistency and trust with absolute nature. Any aspect of nature can be defined in two terms: in terms of absolutes and in terms of perceptions. Absolutes determine the nature of something; this presupposes that there is indeed an objective universe in which the observer exists. On the other hand, perceptions are the aspects of the object or event that present themselves in some meaningful way to the observer. Although the observer may never know the complete or absolute nature of any event, he can be certain the event is valid in some way. His partial assimilation of it enables him to deal with it. He composes an image of the object or event and bases his actions on his perception. The presumption is that the perception is enough from which to make some meaningful decision and consequent action.

Perceptions can be explored and explained, but never in absolute terms. No perception or compilation of perceptions is complete. If I look at a chair, I see something meaningful. I see an object I know can be applied in a useful context. Although I cannot see the actual atoms of that chair in detail, I derive enough useful information from my perception to use the object. I do not know the absolute nature of the chair, but my perception is enough on which to base actions. Furthermore, because I can perceive certain consistencies in that chair and relate them to others, I am able to conceive of something that applies to all chairs—the quality of "chair-ness", if you will. I know that whenever my body is tired, I can look for a chair, and upon finding one, sit down and rest. In human terms, perceptions of reality become reality. We tend to accept objects only in terms of their expected behavior.

This idea of expected behavior is based on the laws of consistency.

If something is never perceived as behaving a certain way, it is difficult to think of it in those terms. Perceptions, then, are very habit-forming. This is a natural response to what is for us an essential way of interacting with our environment. We not only come to accept our perceptions as being real, but eventually to accept them as being complete. It is this latter tendency that causes us problems when we are confronted with totally new data.

Consider another example. If you strike a tuning fork, you do not look for sound waves. You look for vibrations, and wait to hear sound waves. You do not waste time looking for things your senses will not allow you to perceive. You immediately begin collecting perceptions in meaningful terms. You impose your past experience on the event, knowing that the vibrations will cause the tuning fork to appear in several places at once. You are not tricked into believing there are several turning forks; that is, you "edit" the experience in terms of your past experiences. You do not see the sound waves passing through the air, but you have learned to accept that this is how they travel. Your perception in the end is based as much on supposition and interpretation as any one physical event. Your consciousness uses an amalgam of perceptions, assumptions, and interpretations to construct an image, which you presume to be more or less true to the absolute event.

These self-constructed images of reality are in fact your only true knowledge. You have no way of knowing whether your perceptions really reflect the absolute nature of a chair or tuning fork. You only know how they appear to you and how you can use them to your advantage. Your world view is shaped by your perceptions and unswervingly guided by your ability to test the truths you discover.

Testing truth is something each of us does continuously. At every moment of waking consciousness, the human mind is struggling to define what is most critical to it for that moment. This analysis is largely submerged; we do not fully realize how much the mind analyzes the elements of environment acting upon it. If we did, we would likely fall into a paralytic confusion, failing to cope with the great bombardment of data we normally adjust to automatically.

The mind is not the only level of consciousness that has to cope with many external realities. Human consciousness has many levels, each level interacting with its external environment in its own way. Indeed, as we have discovered in our waking state, one level of consciousness may be oblivious to the mechanisms of another. For the most part, we view the waking mind as an individual consciousness, even though that consciousness is governed by other levels. This point of view is the result of our perception of what we are as individuals; it is an interpretation of reality, not reality itself.

Human consciousness is a living potpourri of senses, emotions, thoughts, and imaginings. It accepts and rejects parts of its experience at will. It may partially integrate an experience through one level of consciousness and reject it with another. The reaction depends on specific needs; many of these needs rest in levels of awareness totally foreign to our familiar waking consciousness. Our waking day is largely driven by our corporeal needs. When hungry, we seek food. When in danger, we forget our hunger and attend to survival. And when living in flesh, we submerge the awareness of the base soul.

What we regard as our normal waking state is really only a bound awareness struggling to find its way. The nature of the corporeal body imposes limitations we seek to overcome as souls. The soul itself is subject to limitations imposed by its environment. In the best interests of the moment, certain sacrifices of awareness are always made. As animals living in a specialized biological ecosystem, we are peculiarly oriented to a specific need: to maintain the effectiveness of the corporeal organism. In short, our animal nature demands that we focus on the elements of this world so that the corporeal organism survives. The trade-off is one of degree: how much sacrifice of awareness is necessary, and how much is lack of organized utilization.

Although most people do not need to worry about survival at every waking moment, corporeal needs are cared for first. This is not to say there are no altruistic motives, or selfless people. It only means that at the most basic level, any living consciousness must be utterly devoted to its own self-continuance. Otherwise, it has no self with which to offer aid and succor to others. Also, the need for self-continuance, for survival, is a deeper motivation than the survival of the corporeal body. The body can be shed at will in the interests of the soul. Suicide and death in this world are not always as tragic as we think; they are often evidence of the soul's will to advance to something new. Only through a broader understanding of the soul and its environment can we facilitate our development to the greatest possible degree.

For example, we can't achieve the superb levels of precision in our rational thought that we achieve through instinctive reaction. Autonomous nervous reactions are more precise still. To "think through" a problem such as how to move the arm in response to a burning sensation would take far too long, resulting in a bad burn. At the same time, we use our intellect to a degree not matched by other life in this world. As a result, our instincts are dulled. Our survival has been increasingly mechanized; many native human abilities are now little used. As Carl Jung so revealingly put it, our deeper levels of consciousness are, to our waking minds, the "unconscious".

Somewhat compensatorily, we have developed many techniques for enhancing our powers of consciousness. Some of these are as common as institutional education, social training, and self-discipline. Others are more esoteric, such as meditation, hypnosis, and biofeedback training. Still, we recognize that we don't get as much from our waking awareness as we should. That recognition has led us to explore our consciousness as we do our environment, and to discover that our consciousness is truly a part of that environment. We have only to fully understand how.

To understand ourselves we cannot depend on either an internal or an external quest. We exist as we do primarily because the environment has shaped us. But on a very intrinsic level, we have also shaped our own existence. To some degree, *we* have made us as we are. It is this mix of internal and external activity that defines our individual lives. We are a contact point between consciousness and nonconsciousness, a focus of experience which grows in terms of self-direction and understanding. As living entities, we take more and more control over our environment.

All these limitations point to an inescapable conclusion: that we are in no position to know or understand *everything* about our environment. At best, we can know about portions of our environment that we can perceive or devise machines to perceive. And yet if we have no idea that something is there, we have no need to deal with it or devise a machine to find it. We therefore ignore it.

The end result is that the vastness of our universe escapes our corporeal understanding. We do not view the universe as consisting of many unperceived levels of universe in addition to our perceived cosmos because we have learned that unperceived things often have little direct bearing on our well being. It is not necessary, even, to fully believe in other planes within our own level of universe, because they, too, are usually unperceived. We like to interact with what we can see; if something cannot be seen, we resist believing it is really there. It has taken science thousands of years to overcome such prejudice regarding very familiar atomical events, and even science resists accepting events that do not fit within its own established paradigms.

The universe is broader than man will ever know. As an infinite entity, we cannot ever hope to understand it in absolute terms. Yet we can make our assessments of it more and more viable, and less subjective. We must accept that we have a strong orientation towards perceiving the universe through corporeal eyes, but that this orientation can be adjusted. The first step is to look beyond our atomical plane, to look to the other planes of the Material Level. Then, one step at a time, we can broaden our paradigm of universal order.

Chapter Eleven
UNIVERSAL ORDER

Given our native abilities and the native organization of the universe, how should we view universal order? Is there any way we can forge some bond between our perceptions and the absolute nature of the universe? I think there is. This process of definition is already underway through our sciences. Although our scientific analysis of nature is not perfect, it moves towards divorcing our *interpretations* of our perceptions from the perceptions themselves. We just have to refine and continue this process in a nonatomical context.

The modern mindset is very much governed by the scientific method. This is a philosophy as much as a method, because it guides the actual *way* we must think if we are to be deemed as operating in scientific terms. It therefore imposes certain limits on our ability to interpret nature. Also, because the pure sciences focus nearly exclusively on atomical phenomena, they also determine to a large extent *what* we may think about scientifically. We derive our most objective understandings of nature from the pure sciences, and this unfortunately restricts us to an exploration of atomical nature. It ignores nonatomical events because it cannot control them experimentally.

The scientific method holds that objectivity can be enforced at the human level through experimentation and logical thought. While this presumption is valid in many respects, we often tend to forget that our experiments and logic are based for the most part on our terrestrial experience—that is to say, on atomically based experience. We readily accept the fact that every human investigator brings to his study his own personal biases and history; we tend, however, to forget that our entire culture has a particular bias and history. Our sciences, being founded primarily in a Christian historical context, retain many of the biases and assumptions rooted in Christian theology. Western resistence to the concept of reincarnation is an example; because reincarnation is not central to Christian doctrine, Western scientists—predominantly Christian—have for the most part ignored reincarnation as a valid scientific study. And, as the Western scientific method is adopted in other cultures, many historical prejudices are passed on with it.

There is no such thing in our world as true objectivity. Culturally, Western belief systems are no more objective than those of any other culture. It just happens that the Industrial Revolution of the West devised tools and mechanisms that aid us in objectifying our understanding of nature. These tools help us to determine what we can safely call facts. At the same time, these tools only detect and measure atomical phenomena. Is it any wonder, then, why we often fail to consider that there may be more to the universe than the atomical cosmos?

There is much within the universe that is nonatomical. We may hesitate to accept this in formal scientific terms, but we must at least accept the *possibility* that this is so. Unfortunately, until science and technology become vastly more sophisticated than they are currently, there is no way such a statement can be substantiated. At the moment, there are few organized efforts to reach beyond the atomical cosmos. Parapsychology, investigations of the near-death phenomenon, and a few other disciplines (none of which are viewed as mainstream sciences) are plodding forward. However, these investigations have little focus and virtually no effective technical support. They consequently have little to offer in terms of hard-nosed explanations of the phenomena they investigate. They succeed only in documenting the existence of the phenomena themselves. And until recently society has been quite stubborn about accepting this work.

Perhaps the only nonatomical phenomenon we can hope to analyze and explain scientifically in the near future is that of nonterrestrial contact, or mediumship. We can always assume that thought, precognition, telepathy, and other events of consciousness are totally derived from our atomical organisms; after all, they do involve the brain. However, if we can prove telepathy exists in a human context, we can perhaps also determine that it exists in a nonhuman, nonterrestrial context. This is paramount to proving the existence of our gods.

There are no terms in which we can conceive of our gods being residents of our atomical cosmos. If we do not accept them as having physical validity in nonatomical terms, we can only accept them as being events of imagination, that is, unreal. To believe in God or in gods (as the majority of people still do) is to believe in some alternate system of reality. One of the fundamental teachings of religion is that man is part of a broader community than terrestrial earth. We may choose to diminish this historical message because of our focus on atomical reality, but I think to do so is our loss. The message recurs throughout the world, and I believe the reason it does is that it is substantially correct. We intuitively recognize at a surface level what we already know in the base levels of consciousness.

Westerners find it desirable to separate scientific matters from what might be called spiritual matters. Just as we separate Church and State, we separate scientific quests from spiritual quests. Generally speaking, Westerners are very careful not to believe too strongly in *physical* effects of divine influence, preferring to view them as supernatural. To do otherwise would mean our scientific paradigm has gaping holes and most of us are very uncomfortable with that thought. We therefore practice our spiritual quest in very controlled circumstances, usually within the mainstream churches. To do otherwise still invites social rejection, condescension, and disdain. Consequently there is an almost underground acceptance of many metaphysical beliefs that do not fit in with either mainstream Christian churches or mainstream sciences. According to a 1981 Gallup Poll, some 23 percent of adult Americans—nearly one quarter of the population— believe in reincarnation. Yet reincarnation does not find its way into American social institutions, or become a favored subject of university or government research.

This extent of belief is surprising considering that many metaphysical questions have been actively suppressed. They certainly haven't been broadly supported by mainstream institutions. The success of our sciences in describing atomical phenomena is based on a long history of trial and error. Science has come a long way, and has done so because of the resources dedicated to the quest. If similar resources were dedicated to metaphysical questions, undoubtedly significant progress would be made in these areas as well. Until then, the advance of science in metaphysical areas will be painfully slow.

Just as scientific paradigms have changed continuously, so have religious beliefs. No doctrine is static over time, all being continuously revised to reflect current ideas, political interests, and so on. What changes most, however, are the specific interpretations of doctrine, as opposed to fundamental tenets. No one challenges the universality and validity of such ideas as love, brotherhood of mankind, or mutual support through community effort. What must face daily challenge are the particular practices and mythologies of historical doctrines.

Scientific investigation provides facts that we can use to reinterpret our historical doctrines. Genesis, for example, tells us the world was created in six days. Archbishop Ussher decided a few centuries ago that the geneologies of the Bible placed the date of that Creation in the year 4004 B.C. One wonders if the Archbishop would have said the same thing if he had the benefit of modern geological data. Yet his interpretation of the Bible was widely accepted until better data became available. While a few fundamentalist Christian sects still hold to the Archbishop's idea, most people accept instead the scientific record. We are usually willing to rethink longstanding ideas given sufficient scientific data; sometimes it just takes us a while.

Our acceptance of modern science challenges our traditional assumptions about universal order. The earliest human assumptions about the origins of man and the cosmos were intuitive guesses which happened to gain some mythological or theological significance. Genesis can be used equally effectively to support the Big Bang theory as Archbishop Ussher's ideas. "In the beginning God created the heavens and the earth. The earth was without form and void . . ." These sentences may well describe the universe before the Big Bang. Much of mythology has a heart of truth, if ferreted out.

Intuition can indeed point the way to great truths. Intuitive assessment of perceptions is the native human means of understanding the environment. Until the advent of science, we had no other way of making sense of the environment, of understanding the *why* of things. When empirical explanations are lacking, we always fall back on imagination, even in science. In science we call imagination "speculation" or "hypothesis". When facts fail us, we fill the gaps with our best guesses.

As science develops, it replaces our guesswork with actual facts and tested theory. Theories may still be off-base, but for a hypothesis to formally graduate to the status of theory, it must be tested and shown to be basically sound. This means that many intuitional doctrines of our religions related to physical nature have been disproved by science. Although we still find we need our religions for spiritual succor, we have generally turned away from them in terms of setting the pace for cultural evolution. Science and technology have taken over that role.

Unfortunately, we have also found that science and technology lack the spiritual core of our religions. Our notions of spirituality have become divorced from the mainstream of modern society, and we feel weaker for it. We desire spiritualism—as is evidenced by the great resurgence of fundamentalism, the proliferation of new cults and religions, and the pursuit of many more esoteric mystic philosophies— but we are generally unable to integrate it effectively into modern life. Because of science and technology and the rise of industrial society, human spirituality has become a tandem pursuit, not an integral part of our lives. This is a sad development.

There is little true sharing in these two human quests. We view our material pursuits in a different context than our spirituality. Yet *all* of man's spiritual beliefs have grown out of our interpretations of physical reality. The fact that many of our interpretations have been wrong only points out the need for careful research. To believe in God is not wrong; we just do not have any idea of what God is. There is no question that belief in God (and gods) remains a crucial part of human society; and yet there is no meaningful research I am aware of that scientifically investigates what God may be. In many crucial ways, we are weakened by the reluctance of science and technology to pursue anything traditionally viewed in a religious context. This includes the idea of a soul.

Our historical perspective has led us to talk about the soul as being somehow separate from physical nature because it is certainly separate from the physical nature *that we know in scientific terms*. This situation is the result of a number of factors, but most of all because of our historical cultural predispositions and prejudices. Because the idea of a soul that survives bodily death cannot be easily integrated into current physical theory, science tends to ignore the issue. Although this situation may have evolved quite naturally, there is no reason to hold to it. We can explore the physical nature of the soul and the worlds of our gods in the purest of scientific terms. All it takes is the will to change the way we think. The sooner we realize this, the sooner we will enlarge our world view.

Even though science is more eager to seek out the elemental nature of atoms than that of the soul, the quests are ultimately one and the same. To find the base matter of an atom is to find the base matter of the soul. Atoms and souls are just different expressions of the base matter energy. In terms of their outward characteristics, atoms and souls behave very differently, but they are both manifestations of matter energies.

The study of component parts is a reductionist mode of thought that results in a paradigm of a whole based on the sum of its parts. We can view all of nature in terms of parts; the same set of parts can be recombined in many ways to create vastly different entities. Ultimately, the entire universe can be conceptually reduced to the simplest terms: universal energy. From that single source comes every organized form in the universe. Each level of universe has its base or lowest common denominator, and each progressively higher order of organization has a common denominator shared by a layer of interacting parts. These parts can be viewed as building blocks, each set of building blocks being responsible for a particular subset of nature.

Consider the 105 known atomic elements. Atoms form a working subset of nature. Each atom has its own specific properties, but all share four basic forces. They also share a common set of subatomic particles. No matter how different one atomic element is from another— as different as are gold, lead, mercury, and hydrogen gas—each atom is constructed from similar subatomic particles. They differ only in their respective quantities and combinations of these subatomic particles.

Together, the 105 types of atoms (actually fewer, because some are not known to occur naturally and must be man-made) comprise the cosmos as we know it. Hydrogen is the simplest type of atom, consisting of a single proton and electron. Because it is the simplest atom, there are more hydrogen atoms in the cosmos than any other type. As the simplest atom, it is also the lightest; other types of atoms are made by fusing hydrogen atoms together, such as in the nuclear fires of a star. A star is largely a compact mass of furiously burning hydrogen atoms, the electrons and protons becoming separated from each other to produce a free-floating mass of particles physicists call plasma. Protons are much heavier than electrons and when fused together form the nucleus of an atom. The number of protons fused together in a nucleus determines the type of atom.

Because protons have a positive charge and electrons a counter-balancing negative charge, a nucleus tends to attract an equal number of electrons as it has protons. Nature imposes a symmetry on atomic elements, and rounds it out with a third type of particle—neutral in charge—called a neutron. A neutron is similar to a proton, and in fact neutrons can be converted to protons and vice versa by changing yet another sublayer of particles, the quarks. Hydrogen is the only atomic element not equipped with neutrons. While both protons and neutrons are composed of quarks, physicists still consider electrons to be indivisible. There are also other subatomic particles, some of which are known to be divisible and some not. These particles comprise the cosmos.

Once formed through nuclear action, atoms combine with each other chemically to form molecules. A few atomic elements, such as gold, are chemically nonreactive. Most, however, are reactive to varying degrees. This reactivity is expressed according to very precise rules, imposing a high degree of order on our physical environment. Your body, your house, the air, everything you can touch, smell, or taste is built of molecules. Each and every molecule is formed according to very specific chemical principles. The creative potential of the 105 atoms is virtually limitless. Our organic bodies, for example, are constructed of an array of biochemical molecules that perform astounding feats. Each cell carries a genetic code that is the blueprint for the whole body. Somehow, these molecules are organized under the direction of conscious energy that enables them to function autonomously as an organic structure.

Thus, order arises progressively through various layers of components or building blocks of nature. Each layer, from the quarks, neutrinos, electrons, and other seemingly indivisible particles to the complex molecular structures of the macroscopic world, offers a potentially infinite range of creativity. It just happens that a combination of forces exists that has resulted in a more or less fixed set of parts at any given layer of organization. These parts then govern the types of activity that can occur at the next layer of organization.

Science will eventually trace the component elements of our cosmos below the level of quarks, neutrinos, electrons, and so on. The base matter energy can be described as a basic particle (or waveform) that forms all the higher orders of material organization. Below the level of the base matter energy is the universal energy. Below that, nature seems to peter out into the formless void of the universal force, where action and reaction no longer exist. There is only existence, or not-existence, depending on how you choose to think of it. You might choose to call this primary manifestation "nothing", to say that the universe is an infinitely complex entity formed from nothing. I choose to call it the universal force. How something can be both "something" and "nothing" may seem to us an unresolvable paradox, but at its most elementary state of being, this is the essence of the universe. Both our sciences and our mystic traditions point us to this conclusion.

I have already mentioned Genesis, which describes the universe as being created out of nothing. Science similarly tackles the universal paradox, touching it most closely with its concept of forces. To date, four atomic forces have been identified, the strong and weak nuclear forces, gravity, and electromagnetism. To better visualize and work with the fuzzy world of subatomic forces, physicists have extended the concept of particle to forces. The concept of particles may not be completely accurate in describing such activity, but is so far the most useful tool we have to help us grasp what occurs at that level of reality. Physicists may therefore talk about gravitons as being the particles responsible for gravity, W and Z particles being responsible for the weak nuclear force, the gluon being responsible for the strong nuclear force, and photons being responsible for electromagnetism. Together these four forces form the essence of atomical nature; without them atoms would not be able to cohere as units. They are believed to have an underlying unity that represents some superforce; already, all but gravity have been demonstrated to be unified through the Grand Unified Theory. Essentially, I am saying that such a conceptual model can be carried to even greater degrees of unification, ultimately to the universal force itself.

We can also apply the idea of particle physics to other planes. If atoms are the basic building blocks of the cosmos, we can be certain that there are similar building blocks underlying all the other material planes. The Material Level's fundamental mode of operation is based on particles, whatever form these particles truly have. Our plane represents one field of activity within the broader field of our level of universe. It, in turn, is just a part of the universal field. Each layer can be described as an order of organization, each order having its own basic field of operation.

This concept of orders of organization can be used to classify universal order. It allows us to talk about various steps or building blocks in the construction of nature. In these terms, the universal energy can be viewed as the first order of organization. It is the first layer of organized substance in the universal field. The various levels of universe, of which the Material Level is one, represent a second order of organization. Within our particular level of universe, planes are a third order of organization. And so on. We can define orders of organization however it suits the best scientific data of the day; this provides us with a tool that can integrate many vastly disparate types of reality in a single overall paradigm. Whatever science discovers can be systematically identified and classified, regardless of how foreign it is to some other aspect of nature. Rather than disregard valid data, as science has to date in regards to the existence of the soul and certain nonterrestrial events, unexplained phenomena can be incorporated into the overall paradigm on the understanding that not every piece has to fit at all times. The paradigm always assumes the existence of unknown aspects of nature.

Such concepts as levels of universe and orders of organization will become more important as science evolves. For the present, science has only seriously concerned itself with classifying atomical nature. Someday, however, science will expand its investigation to include a study of neighboring planes and, more vigorously, the human soul. I don't believe science will forever be so fascinated by all things atomical that it will not seriously consider the possibility of the soul's survival of bodily death. When it does, it will by corollary be forced to explore what happens to the soul when it separates from the body. This will become the study of the Afterlife, and eventually the study of other planes.

As long as our consciousness is our only true receptor for events and realities external to the atomical plane, we will have trouble integrating our spiritual philosophies with our material world. We will still hesitate to accept the soul as a physical entity, or to seek out a material or physical basis for the guidance we see as coming from God or other divine powers. We are perhaps afraid we will disprove some of our cherished but ancient beliefs. But I think that even though we will eventually prove many of our *interpretations* of ancient teachings to be wrong, we will prove their *essence* to be true. There is a God, a Creator of All that Is. This is the universal consciousness itself; and there are gods who guide each of us daily, who intercede in our lives. These, too, are discoverable, just as we can discover the material basis of the soul. We must remember that all mythology, whether religious or secular, has at its heart some truth. But whenever we are not prepared to change our views, we impede our spiritual growth.

Our lives, though dependent on the human body to provide certain conversions of energy, are not totally dependent on this corporeal form. We could as easily have evolved to use another form in another place. That we haven't only indicates that our past includes a particular set of events that has led to our current state. We now continue to evolve in a direction determined by these causative events. We have chosen as a task the unravelling of our history. If we are to be true to our quest, we must be prepared to go wherever the quest leads. If it leads to the reformation of our historical assumptions, our interpretations of reality, or our religious beliefs, so be it.

I believe our quest for spiritual succor can aid us in driving our materially oriented sciences. By reaching out to our guides, we can set the stage for a final acceptance of other worlds and the entities who dwell there. Our guides have always influenced the development of science as well as our spiritual doctrines. Eventually, their guidance will press us on into some factual analysis of their existence. Our final acceptance of them will occur when we find some way of translating the essentially nonsensory experience of mediumship and other non-terrestrial events into sensory experiences. We will then know once and for all that man is not alone in this universe as a higher intelligence.

Chapter Twelve
THE GUIDES OF MAN

As a race of souls, the Guides of Man are similar to us in many ways. They too incarnate in a plane that provides them with objective experiences, very much as we do on terrestrial earth. They also have an Afterlife, though it is a different plane than ours. Yet they are also different from us in many ways. They are more evolved than we are, having lived longer and used more planes for their development.

The guides perform a vital role in our individual and cultural development. Through their often dynamic interaction with us, which at times spills over from the base levels of consciousness into surface levels, we have been led to pursue our highest ideals. It is no wonder that to primitive peoples—and to many people in our most technologically advanced cultures—they seem to be gods.

Their relationship with us is established at the base levels of consciousness, through the base soul. They are older souls, more evolved and more skilled in the arts of life. Human souls are relatively young souls, not far along in their development, but far enough so that we can begin tackling some of the higher ideals of life. Our efforts are somewhat hampered by our choice of evolutionary plane, as terrestrial earth is not as conducive to the soul's evolution as many other planes, including the worlds of our guides. For example, terrestrial earth requires vast amounts of energy to sustain the most elementary functions of life. The dense matter energies that form atomical nature are not as easily manipulated as the matter of other planes.

The very matter of our plane therefore resists being turned to our purposes. But we do overcome many barriers to progress and develop ever higher forms of civilization. As souls, we use a biological species that has evolved a particular type of intelligence that allows the development of civilizations. Humanity represents a transition from the simple biological evolution of most plant and animal life to a higher focus of life. Because civilization is new to this plane, many of its principles are borrowed from other worlds, among them the worlds of our guides.

We are working their teachings into our world in many ways. We emulate their culture however we can, given the physical differences between our worlds. At the level of the base soul, we are familiar with their ways and attempt to apply them here. Obviously, the transplanting of such nonterrestrial culture is not entirely successful, but enough survives and is adapted so that we understand and implement in rudimentary terms many high ideals.

Such teachings as love, honor, and brotherhood can take root in even the harshest of circumstances. We adapt the expression of these ideals to the physical conditions of our world. For example, we express love biologically, its physical root existing in the nature of the biological animal that we are. Yet biological love is just one manifestation of universal love. There are many types of love in our world, and not all love is restricted to human beings.

There is no doubt that other mammals experience forms of primal love. Biological love is evident in the care given by a mother to her young; and who really doubts that a dog loves his master. In humans there is also romantic love, love of nature, and love of ideals and ideas. Each of these forms of love has roots in both the biological world and soul-worlds. Love itself—universal love—is an underlying theme of all our religions and spiritual beliefs, which largely originate in the teachings of the Guides of Man.

Our expressions of universal love are adaptations made necessary by first what is possible within our physical circumstances and second by what is possible considering our current human abilities. We love as our environment enables us to love. As a biological entity, the human organism has a set of abilities and physical needs. Any soul that joins such a vehicle brings with it its own set of abilities and needs. There is a marriage of abilities and needs, and the result is a unique individual—a soul joined with a body. The individual then proceeds to act within his environment to the best of his abilities. If a trait such as love is involved, it can be experienced at all levels of being, in many potential ways.

At the biological level, we use such characteristics as love to enhance our chances for survival; no human child, the most helpless young on earth, would survive without the single-minded devotion of its mother or other care-giver. Similarly, we turn many other ideals to useful purposes in enhancing our survival and the quality of our lives. Yet the selection of love as a biological tool bears the mark of our soul-nature. It is something our type of life-entity incorporates into its evolution. Many other species, such as most reptiles, do not provide any maternal care of their young or show any other form of love, rudimentary or otherwise. They use other techniques to ensure the survival of their species, some species having been successful for more than 100 million years.

In our world, biological species and life-entities such as souls combine to create unique forms of life. Neither the biological entity nor the life-entity entirely determines the characteristics of a species, but rather they share in combining their traits in a new life, an active synergy that results in something never seen before. If the life-entity brings with it love or some other characteristic, the biological organism provides a physical context in which that characteristic can be expressed. Our particular choice of ideals and methods of expressing them are always influenced by our guides. This influence extends not just to the selection of an individual corporeal body for a single incarnation, but an entire evolutionary course, through many types or classes of vehicle. Our course, though currently set for this world, will be guided through other worlds as well. In the meantime, we learn from the vehicle to which we are currently committed.

Souls interact with the flesh understanding that they not only shape to some small degree the flesh, but that the flesh shapes *their* evolution to a very large degree. A vehicle such as the human organism provides structure and foundation for the soul's evolution, pointing the soul to a defined range of evolutionary possibilities. This range exists for the soul-race as well as the individual, each individual adding its bit to the collective evolution of both the soul-race and, to a lesser extent, the biological organism.

The evolution of any species bears the marks of many races and orders of life-entity. The ascent of man, as anthropologists call our biological evolution, is a path shared by a series of soul-races of which ours is merely the most recent. Our species is not some final product of evolution, as people are often tempted to view it, but simply a very successful experiment of nature. Our soul-race guides the species for now, as other races guided our biological ancestors. Thus, our biology shows the cumulative effect of not just millennia of biological evolution, but also the mark of myriad races of life-entity. A species often experiences significant biological variation when a new soul-race takes it over. The life-entity, then, *inspires* biological variations in Darwinian terms. In other words, environment presents a range of possibilities and the life-entity guides the organismic evolution in selecting particular responses.

As Darwin stated, biological evolution is based on existing species changing gradually until they become different species. All biological species in our world originated from a single form of proto-life which eventually developed into single-celled life capable of procreation through division. These first forms of terrestrial life in time evolved into all the plants and animals of the modern world.

Although Darwin pointed out that environment presents challenges of survival to each lifeform that it meets through selective variation, he failed—as do evolutionary theorists to this day—to answer *why* a particular selection is favored over other potential selections. The gentle giraffe, for instance, has obviously opted for a long neck so that it can browse on high leaves. Yet the elephant, also a leaf-eater, has developed into a powerful creature with a long, sinuous trunk. It can just as easily uproot a tree to get at its leaves as delicately pluck them one by one with the end of its trunk. It is not surprising that animals use their natural skills to get food, but why does one species develop a long neck and another a long nose? Why so many different ways of dealing with the same environments? What motivates the selection of particular reactions to particular stimuli? The answers, I suggest, are to be found in the living energy of the life-entity itself.

The influence of the life-entity at the biological level is three-fold. First, it has a physical effect because of the joining of the unique type of life-energy with a unique organism; this is at the level of pure physical reactivity. This is particularly pronounced when a new race of souls begins using a vehicle, resulting in many biological variations. Second, a life-entity can influence biological evolution by guiding the behavior of the individual. If sufficient numbers of individuals modify behavior in a similar way, the behavior is eventually encoded in the gene pool over a number of generations. This is the Darwinian form of selective evolution and can be seen indisputably in operation in all the forms of selective breeding practiced by man with his domestic animals. Third, life-entities in our level of universe are material entities and can influence the makeup of the flesh through deliberate manipulations of atomical energy. This is a fully conscious form of activity, a sort of "mind over matter", or more appropriately stated as life-energy matter influencing atomical energy matter.

External entities can also influence biological evolution in any of these three general ways. Our guides have had a significant influence in human evolution in these terms. Their work is ultimately aimed at the careful engineering of the soul-order Man. Although many of us may recoil at that thought, we should note that we similarly guide the development of our own children as we try to mold them into productive members of society. Our guides' goal is similar, to serve the colonization of this world with intelligent beings and civilizations. They sometimes act directly on us, but more often indirectly by guiding us as soul-entities, instilling in us certain desires that lead us on in the quest for higher civilizations.

The soul-order Man (capitalized man) refers to more than just the Human Race of souls or the biological species man. It does include the Human Race, but also all other soul-races in a direct line of evolution towards joining human flesh. These are races currently using less-evolved mammalian species; of course, this means I am holding that a single soul uses progressively more sophisticated species as it evolves. This evolution is always progressive, never regressive. In other words, a human soul will not be reincarnated as a mouse for wrongs committed in this life, but it does mean it has used many species as evolutionary vehicles, including rodents such as mice.

The Order of Man also includes a higher race of souls, souls that have moved on from this terrestrial plane altogether. These souls are in a transitionary phase, preparing for a higher order of experience. They, too, are guided by the Guides of Man, and dwell on a specific plane one step higher in the hierarchy of matter energies comprising our planet Earth. They have completed their incarnations within human bodies and are now working on the next phase of their evolution. They are our Great Souls, the souls of our race who have done so well on earth that they no longer need to reincarnate here.

The evolution of a life-entity such as a soul is much faster than biological evolution. This is why races of souls come and go while only very slight changes occur in the host biological species. Souls evolve as the result of experience, growing as rapidly as they are physically able to digest what they learn with each passing incarnation. Biological organisms, on the other hand, change very slowly, with each generation producing only very minor variations. Most of these variations are not sustained through future generations. Some species, such as cockroaches and crocodiles, have changed very little over many millions of years. Our species has evolved very quickly in comparison, but still evolves at a snail's pace in relation to the speed at which an individual soul evolves.

In essence, then, souls graduate from a specific type of evolutionary vehicle when they are ready. Eventually, an entire soul-race evolves beyond the need for a particular vehicle and moves on. Another race moves in to take its place. At present, our soul-race is in its heyday with the species of man, though a few individual souls outgrow the race as we go. Someday, the race as a whole will outgrow the species, and will migrate en masse to the next plane over a period of several centuries. We will then continue to evolve using a new type of vehicle on a higher plane.

The concept of a soul or life-entity that survives the flesh resolves some of the problems remaining in Darwinism. It not just answers the question of what motivates species to select certain responses, but gives us a broader view on the origins of life, something Darwinism does not explain.

Darwinism doesn't tell us what life is, or how it came to be. We know the general history of biological evolution, and how it has populated this world from the many forms of single-celled life to the great blue whale. But we do not know where the originating spark of life came from or how it came to inhabit biological compounds. We know only that biological species support and sustain life, and can pass on from generation to generation, creating new biological forms in the process.

Science offers as its best guess that life somehow originated in the primordial seas of terrestrial earth. This seems likely from the point of view that organic compounds can be formed through electrical processes such as would have been present then; this much has been verified in laboratories, and similar compounds have been discovered in meteorites falling to earth from outer space. Yet this only indicates the creation of biological compounds, not life itself. We don't know how these compounds became imbued with life, or how to take these nonliving amino acids and make them live.

However, if we consider that a life-entity can exist separately from the organic body, then we suddenly don't have to find the origins of *life* in the early terrestrial seas, but only the origins of biochemistry. And that much we have established already. We still, however, are left with the question of where life—separate from the body or otherwise—really came from.

My guides suggest that it originated in another plane according to processes analogous to the formation of the first organic compounds. Life-energy came from near-life; then through a process of colonization of the various planes, life was implanted in the early organic compounds of the terrestrial seas. The prehistoric transfer of life from another plane to this one was quite a natural phenomenon, occurring according to principles still used by more sophisticated life today. I know this is not a complete answer, but it adds one more piece to the puzzle. I believe it is an idea worth considering, especially since I think it will eventually be proved to be true.

Life, then, didn't actually form on this plane so much as adapt to suitable structures that naturally occurred here. This also fits what we know of life; it adapts wherever and however it can to make use of even the most hostile environments. Undoubtedly there were many failures before life truly took hold on our plane. Yet a successful organism did evolve to become the biological forebear of every species extant today. Now, with the ascent of man, the impetus of earthly evolution is no longer directed at merely establishing life on terrestrial earth, but to develop higher forms of life, life that can pursue civilization, love, and many other high ideals.

We may pause to wonder why whole worlds are mobilized to pursue civilization or any other ideal. But this is like wondering why life itself exists. All we can say is that we are alive, and we are engaged in the progressive development of civilizations. None we have created so far is perfect, and none will survive forever. Yet each serves the evolution of its members, and the progression of evolution is a goal in itself. This may not be the definitive meaning of life that you seek, but it is a goal common to all of us. Furthermore, we are guided in this goal in every aspect of our lives.

The influence of our guides is most evident in our religions. A single human, properly guided, and in the right place and time, can have an extraordinary effect on the direction of human evolution. We have only to look at history to see the effects of the teachings of such men as Christ, Mohammed, and Prince Sidharta, who became the Buddha.

Although such individuals are often lionized as gods, they are men who teach men. Their profound teachings do, however, derive from a higher source. They teach as their own personal guides lead them. They teach universal truths in a context accessible by human beings, their successes and failings just further proof that their exalted state arises from the truths given them and not their personal being. Yet they represent God the Creator as well, just as each one of us and every living thing does. We are all a part of All that Is.

Each of us has our own guides. When we appeal to our deities, we are answered by our personal guides. When we feel the kiss of fate, often it is our guides. And when we succeed or fail, we often feel the success or failure of our guides, because they are not perfect either. They teach us as best they know, their judgment weighted on greater experience and wisdom, but always subject to their limitations, and to the limitations of their human charges. We can therefore think of our guides as gods, if we wish, for they often present themselves to us as such. But we cannot see them as God the Creator of All that Is, because that is a state of universal being. In the truest terms, God is the infinite universe; the infinite universe is God.

The guides present themselves to us as gods for many reasons. One reason is simply because it impresses us. If you were to bend a wandering people to your will, to influence them in ways they could not see the immediate purpose of, what would you do? You would grab their attention, that's what. And our guides can do that, making us see things that are not there, or moving us to actions that are normally beyond our powers. This can happen today as easily as in Biblical times. How many times have you read of a desperate mother who lifts a car from her child? Such an act requires a magnificent concentration of energy and strength. Although her guides cannot actually lift the car for her, they can certainly help her focus her total consciousness in a way not possible in normal states. Similar focus can be achieved through guided mysticism. As well as imparting knowledge and moral virtue, the guides also seek to teach us ways of strengthening ourselves. Historically, religion has served such a role.

Although man is a cultivated species, we still have much responsibility for our own actions. We are gradually learning to have more control over ourselves and our environment, taking on more and more responsibility for our evolutionary destiny. We have, in fact, achieved the dangerous point of being able to wipe ourselves out while still not having sufficient self-control to be certain that we won't. All the while, our guides steer us into certain channels.

The Guides of Man help organize the development of each individual human soul. We have other guides than just those belonging to the Guides of Man, but these others play a subordinate role. There is a hierarchy of guides, some of whom are involved with the individual for many incarnations. However, each individual human soul has a single guide who is the overall anchor for his development: a senior partner, if you will, in the process of life.

Through their long association with us, the guides gradually turn over to us more control of our lives and evolution. This increasing responsibility is apparent in the incarnations of each individual soul, and collectively in human societies. Each soul gathers a bit more experience with each incarnation and therefore can assume greater responsibilities in its next incarnation. How fast it evolves is up to the soul, given the physical constraints of its environment. Likewise, each society of individuals has an overall rate of evolution, and, just as important, it focuses on specific characteristics. While Western societies have emerged as the dominant cultures of the modern world, we have lost much of our spiritual sensitivity; our reliance on machines has caused us to mistrust our intuitive perceptions. Consequently, we are not only individually less sensitive to our immediate environment, but also to our guides. Although we wish to retain spiritual values in our modern technological cultures, we are not certain how to do so.

A greater sensitivity to the messages rising from within us can help us reestablish a more conscious relationship with our guides in everyday life. Each of us must define personal goals and pursue them. The guides aid in this process at every level of our being. If as a culture we decide to become more spiritually sensitive, the guides will ensure that each individual has an opportunity to cooperate in that venture. If on the other hand we continue as we are, the guides will also continue as *they* are, working at a more subliminal level. Their guidance will be felt in our lives, but only obliquely, as most of us experience it now. It is not necessary for us to be aware of their guidance for it to have an effect in our lives, but if we knowledgeably pursue it, then we can derive even greater benefit. At the very least, it can help each of us feel more self-assured and confident in personal goals. At the most, it can help us come to a broader understanding of our place in the universe, our origins, and our destiny.

Chapter Thirteen

THE ORIGINS OF LIFE
IN THE MATERIAL LEVEL

The Material Level is liberally populated. We may not be scientifically aware of any life except that evident to us on our own terrestrial plane, but the life is there. We may even presume that life exists in other levels of universe, though what form it might have there is anybody's guess. However, we can make fairly safe assumptions about what nonterrestrial lifeforms within our own level might be like. Two divergent areas of human thought provide clues: particle physics and mythology.

Particle physics tells us what to expect of material energies. We know that particles in quantum terms are not solid, but rather more like waveforms. If we accept the idea that material energies, regardless of their manifestation, are essentially particle energies, then we must assume that any lifeform within the Material Level is also composed of particle energies. Life-energy is particle energy, formed from a base substance that is as much a part of each soul as it is each atom. The difference is in how the energies are configured. If we care to trace the nature and quantum mechanics of life-energy, we have to continue our quest into the nature of the atom. At some point we will develop the expertise and technology to measure, quantify, and experiment with actual particles of life-energy.

The second set of clues gives us an idea of what form or behavior life on other planes may have. Human mythology is filled with all sorts of creatures. There are fairies and goblins, nymphs and sirens, gods, devils, and angels. There are mythological half-man, half-beast creatures such as the Minotaur and Centaurs of Greek mythology. Aboriginal peoples throughout the world add thousands of other mythological entities to human lore. While it is unlikely that such entities exist exactly as depicted in mythology, it may well be possible that our imaginative myth-makers were inspired by dreams or actual astral travels to other planes. There may not be fairies with sparkling wands, but there may be entities that resemble the folktale fairies in appearance and action. Similarly, there might be mischievous entities that look and act like goblins; I remember a dream I had in which little goblin-like entities were present, doing mischievous things. It seemed more real that most dreams, as if it were happening during ordinary waking consciousness. This is actually a very special state of awareness between waking and sleeping in which many strange events occur; it is when most people astral project for the first time, and when many people experience direct communications with other planes, some of a very frightening nature.

In Newfoundland, one such event is called "Hag sitting". It involves some oppressive monster-like entity sitting on an unsuspecting sleeper's chest. The victim feels himself to be completely paralyzed, though he believes himself to be fully awake. Finally, with the greatest of effort, the victim manages to twitch a finger and the "Hag" vanishes. This happened to a roommate of mine once, and we spent the next day checking the windows of the apartment for a way such a thing could have gained entrance. Eventually I read about such occurrences, and had my own experience with the goblins. In my half-dream, the goblins were working viciously to saw through my glasses with a dull knife to cut open my head. It seemed terrifyingly real and I was paralyzed until I remembered that I didn't wear my glasses to bed. I was then able to gather up the concentration to twitch just one finger and the goblins disappeared. After a few more such visits, in which I was ready for them, they eventually left me alone. I learned a valuable lesson: that though such events of consciousness are probably real, the actual damage done is psychological, through fear, and not by damage to our organic selves. Still, fear can be real enough, as anyone with the night-terrors can attest.

It is not just malicious creatures that invade our minds when our natural defenses are down. We can communicate with many types of entities, usually entities that are closely related to us in terms of soul-energy structure. This is what makes communications with our guides possible. It is little different than the telepathic communications that happen between us and our friends and relatives in everyday terms. The mechanics of consciousness are such that two people who know one another can contact each other telepathically more easily than strangers. The stronger the bond, the stronger the ability to make telepathic contact. Proximity can also be a factor; experiment by staring at someone's back and time how long it takes the person to turn around. The nonterrestrial lifeforms most immediately apparent to us are those on planes neighboring ours on the scale of matter density.

Planes are organized based on the density of their formative matter energies, ours containing the most dense forms of matter. Because of their proximity to us, entities on these neighboring planes are most likely to contact us. Evidence of this contact often shows up in some of our dream images. When asleep we can contact many different worlds and states of consciousness. Some of these contacts are remembered for what they are, but usually they are twisted and misshapen as they surface through the various levels of consciousness. The result is that we remember dreams and visions of many fantastic forms, some of which may be pure imagination and others quite close to the truth.

Of course, it is difficult to tell which dreamscapes are more real than others when all can be quite fantastic. Yet here we can invoke the powers of consistency. If many peoples in many times have created the same myths, the same legends and have described the same fantastic entities, perhaps there is something to those myths. Fairies, goblins and guardian angels are three recurrent themes that I think have some merit. These are not necessarily entities closely related to us, though some may be. Some may just interact with us because it amuses them. Others take on a task of protecting or guiding particular individuals they have a particular interest in.

Then there are the many types of entity within the framework of this planet that we do not contact, that we have no knowledge or mythology of, and who do not bother to contact us in any way. Each plane is host to a vast panorama of life as amazing in its diversity as that of this plane. All this life, too, can be classified according to taxonomic relationships, a taxonomy of life-energy, if you will. Just as we classify biological forms of life on this terrestrial plane, we can classify all lifeforms according to their inherent life-energy.

As in any taxonomic system, some entities are more closely related than others. However, all life within our planet has arisen from a single source. What form that life took originally is open to conjecture, but someday we can trace backwards from our own life-entity to it in much the same way as we can trace biological evolution back to the microbe that was the biological parent of all species of plant and animal on this plane.

Some cosmic set of events allowed life to emerge within the Material Level, probably before Earth was even formed. Since then it has evolved wherever possible. There is some specific set of forces that spontaneously creates life from nonliving materials; this set of forces has apparently either existed at some point within the formation of our planet, or our planet has been colonized from elsewhere after it formed. Either way, the Material Level possesses now or possessed at one time the ability to spontaneously create life. As far as our planet is concerned, life first appeared on nonterrestrial planes; I suspect it was formed there by the violent activities of our planet in formation. However, before we can make effective investigations of the origins of life in our planet or its widely disparate types of nonterrestrial life, we must have a clear idea of what life is.

Life as we know it is just an extension of universal being. Everything in the universe shares in a universal being that is conscious of itself in every respect. This universal being can be called God: a summation of All that Is, all knowledge, and all that can ever be. This means that atoms are a part of that universal consciousness as much as any living being. In fact, atoms in these terms are alive. They have a life-span, and they have a consciousness at the physical level. Each and every aspect of each and every atom knows exactly what its place is in the universe, and unfailingly responds to every force acting on it. Lifeforms do the same; the only difference is that lifeforms have an additional ability, though limited, in determining *what* their reactions will be. They have, in other words, limited (and varying) degrees of self-direction.

While it is metaphysically correct to say that an atom is alive based on the fact that it shares in the universal consciousness, it is linguistically useful to maintain a distinction between "life" and "nonlife" or "animate" and "inanimate". Lifeforms have the ability to *decide* on actions, whereas inanimate entities such as atoms do not. Though also forced to react to every force acting on them, lifeforms can to a certain extent determine what their reaction will be. Yet they must also respond to physical forces; in that sense, each and every lifeform is an inherent part of the universal consciousness. Each of us, just as our mystics have always taught us, is part of All that Is, a part of God.

The terms life and nonlife, then, distinguish a degree or quality of self-direction, not any fundamental difference in being or substance. Life-energy is not some magical quality that imbues itself within atoms, nor is it some purely electrochemical activity cooked up by body cells. It is a quantum process of its own and is expressed within the Material Level in terms of particle physics. Though we have yet to identify any particular family of life-energy particle, we will eventually do so.

Life, as we know it, is directed at overcoming the second law of thermodynamics. This law, generally speaking, states that all matter must devolve to forms of lesser organization. Life as we know it comprises organizations of matter that are able to defeat this law to some degree. Life organizes energy; nonlife allows its organization of self or integrated being to dissipate. The coherence of an atom, in other words, breaks down over time, whereas a life-entity grows. The life-entity's powers of self-direction enable it to rebuild its deteriorating self with new material energies. A nonliving entity such as a rock does not. The rock merely erodes; in time the very atoms that comprise the rock devolve.

Because life-entities consistently act for their own self-continuance, they have an added characteristic not necessarily shared by inanimate objects. They grow. Or, more precisely put, they evolve. As they take in more nonliving material energies to convert them to more sophisticated life-energies, they become more adept and efficient at converting energies. After a period of evolution, the process takes on new purpose; rather than just continue to exist, the life-entity develops interests, goals, and objectives. It passes from merely wanting to survive to developing higher purpose. It develops ideals. There may be any number of ideals that one life-entity may pursue, and the more varied the environment, the more varied the goals. Yet the common theme is to evolve, to advance one's interests whatever they may be.

To a large extent, the interests of a life-entity are driven by its most immediate environment. Our most immediate environment is this terrestrial earth. Consequently, our most pronounced interests are anchored to this plane. But we don't spend our entire evolutionary cycle here; we spend time in an Afterlife following each incarnation. For these brief periods, our interests are measurably broadened. We take an interest in other planes, explore them, take note of what we experience, and eventually when we return to terrestrial earth we bring these experiences with us, hidden deeply in the base conscious. Some of these memories surface during our terrestrial lives, even though they may not represent a direct interest for the moment. When they do, they may seem out of place, fantastic, or even crazy. But sometimes, they find their way into our folklore, our legends, and even our formalized religions. The life of other planes becomes a part of our world without us always recognizing it. However, we in the industrialized world should remember that to many cultures the spirit worlds are very much close at hand. They recognize the existence of other worlds and integrate them into their everyday lives.

As noted earlier, life within our planet did not originate on the atomical plane. Atomical energies are essentially nonliving energies. Furthermore, the mechanics don't exist on this plane to spontaneously create life. This is why the spontaneous creation of life remains such a mystery to us. However, on other planes the processes are not perceived as being so unusual. Once a suitable multi-plane framework evolves around a suitable atomical entity, life can easily emerge on certain other planes. This is not something that happens on every planet, or even most planets. But it does happen, and has happened elsewhere in the cosmos. Our planet just happens to be hospitable enough to allow life to emerge not just on other planes, but to colonize the terrestrial plane as well.

The Big Bang was essentially a blueprint for all the laws and forces that have emerged within the Material Level. It not only determined that the atomical cosmos should emerge, but also that the multi-plane system around atomical bodies would develop and, similarly, life would evolve. In these terms, every event of the Material Level's evolution has already been determined in physical terms. The future is available to be read in the very make-up of the material energies around us—and in us. More sophisticated lifeforms are able to read these blueprints. At a subliminal level, so are we, and that is why we can experience precognition. However, we can also act to change the future. Because we have a certain degree of self-direction, we can alter some of our personal experiences. We may not ever change the evolutionary direction of the Material Level, but we can control to some extent our personal evolution.

The formation of life-energy is a mechanical process. Our corporeal bodies perform this feat easily, once set to the task by the chance union of some primitive life-energy with the proto-organic molecules of early earth. Life-energy forms from near-life energy. Near-life energy forms from nonliving energies that encounter certain specific forces and catalytic energies. Once nonliving energies are synthesized into near-life energies, it is nearly certain that they will further synthesize into true life-energies. Once a body of life-energy is established, it begins to evolve, and continues to evolve. It takes on its own critical mass, so to speak, and refuses to die.

It remains a mystery even in the soul-worlds as to when and where life first emerged within the Material Level. The assumption can be made that the first lifeforms still live and still evolve. They are undoubtedly very advanced entities indeed, probably far beyond anything we could understand. But we can also assume that they remain lifeforms still dependent on particle energies, that is, they consist of some form of material energy. They may have come to understand much about the universe, but they are probably as much confined within the bounds of the Material Level as we are. Yet that shouldn't be a problem. There is a lot of room in a level of universe.

It is fun to speculate what such sophisticated entities could learn in the course of 10 to 15 billion years, considering what we can learn in three-score-and-ten. And they would be so much more practiced at learning. But what happens beyond the duration of the Material Level? Surely, if a life-entity has existed for billions of years, it must feel the mortality of an environment that is approaching a Big Crunch, which scientists speculate may be as little as 20 billion years away. One wonders if they haven't adopted a strategy for dealing with such an event, if they might even be contemplating controlling—or suspending—it. What properties would a lifeform need to control the Big Crunch? Such a lifeform would seem god-like indeed.

In the course of universal evolution, even the four billion years our planet has existed is an instant. As an infinite construct, the universe exists forever. But everything within it must end. Thus, for life to survive something as cataclysmic as the Big Crunch must necessarily involve the contemplation of either changing the event or changing the self to adapt to the event. Existence on a small scale such as our planet can offer practice for such a future. How many species on our terrestrial plane alone have come and gone? How many lifeforms have used the biological organisms of terrestrial earth to learn the techniques of adaptation, of change in the face of violent upheavals in environment? Each day of our lives is a learning experience, a microcosm of the universal experience. Everything we do, no matter how trivial or insignificant, provides us with a map to the destiny of the universe.

The seas of the universe may ebb and flow from simplicity to complexity and back again, but the whole is always maintained. It exists as it dictates to itself, its internal changes a ferment under perfectly organized control. What we view as an increase in order or disorder is really just our limited view of a universal balancing act. We can see life evolving to ever higher forms, and inanimate energies devolving. Because we don't see the whole picture, we may not be aware of what becomes of one state of organization, or how another arose. But we can be certain of a few key principles, one of which is that life infallibly creates more life.

Life constructs more life by transforming nonliving elements into life-energy. This is very much a physical process. In human terms, it requires the physical properties of more than one plane to complete. This is why we reincarnate. The physical energy of the atomical plane is indeed incorporated into life-energy, requiring several stages to complete.

The first stage is to create near-life particles of energy. This is energy that has the potential of being formed even further into true life-energy. Originally this happened in the early ferment of our level of universe. Now it occurs in many more refined contexts. In human terms, it is begun through the digestive processes of the corporeal body.

The next stage is the formation of the actual particles of true life-energy. The corporeal body also aids in this task, but existing life-energy is also required. The Spirit is constructed of fully formed life-energy; it and the base soul interact with the corporeal body to manipulate the biologically generated near-life energies into true life-energy. This process is sustained from generation to generation through biological birth and the rebirth of souls through reincarnation. A fetus is sustained in the womb not just by the biological nourishment of its mother, but also by the mother's life-energy. When the soul joins the fetus, the third link is available and the new person has the potential of self-sustenance. The processing of near-life energy into life-energy occurs mostly during sleep throughout the corporeal lifetime.

Because life-energy is unstable, it quickly breaks down during normal biological activity. This breakdown is responsible for much of your body heat. The life-energy of the Spirit must therefore be constantly replenished. Just as the corporeal body is reconstituted by the biochemicals of food, the food energy is also precisely woven into the fabric of the Spirit. At no point is the Spirit ever fully anchored to the atomical energy of the flesh. It is free to leave and return, tied to the base soul only by a fragile link of consciousness.

Eventually, the corporeal body dies. The base soul leaves, taking the Spirit with it. Base soul and Spirit, held apart by layers of physical dependency of consciousness and material nature while in flesh, are suddenly merged in the Afterlife. They physically fuse into one entity over a period of time, which is the process of consolidation. This involves a physical transformation of the unstable life-energy to the more stable soul-energy. At the same time, the soul undergoes a private, qualitative assessment of the events and experiences of the recent incarnation in light of past incarnations. After a further process of deciding what its best options and most pressing objectives are, the soul prepares to join a new body. When it finds a suitable opportunity, it joins the flesh for a new incarnation. And the cycle begins again.

Not all lifeforms evolve according to the human pattern. Plants, for instance, do not have defined, individual souls the way animals do. The life-entity of a plant is not geared to specific individuality to the same degree as animal evolution. The life-entities that use plant forms therefore have different priorities of development. Yet the differences between the life-entities of plants and animals are not as great as you might suppose. Although plants and animals diverged from a common ancestor at almost the outset of biological evolution, the material base of their life-entities is quite similar.

The key difference is that an animal is directed by a soul-entity, whereas a plant is not. A soul is a specific construct of life-energies, one that includes a base layer with additional levels providing certain other functions that support the types of self-direction animals exhibit. The life-energy of plants is not organized in the same way, but has many of the same material properties. In fact, the life-energy of the Spirit and that of plants is most similar. These organizations are more fluid, and less defined in terms of individuality. When sperm is kept alive in a frozen state in sperm banks, for example, it is life-energy, not soul-energy, that is present. Each sperm does not represent a little soul, but merely some of the man's own life-energy locked within a living cell. Plant cells operate in much the same way.

Life-entities on other planes exhibit an even broader range of characteristics than they do on terrestrial earth. Although all descended from the original lifeform that appeared within the multi-plane framework of Earth hundreds of millions of years ago, they have all evolved in their own directions since. Some may be closely related to us, such as the Guides of Man. Others are not closely related at all.

Much of the complexity of the multi-plane nature of Earth is actually a result of the many lifeforms resident here. Life is a very catalytic force and causes many sorts of activities on a purely physical level as well as an organizational level. In other words, lifeforms not only reorganize material forms such as we do on our plane, but actually reorganize material energies. Some planes are nearly entirely the products of the consciousness of living entities. Nonliving energies are taken from the sun, from atomical matter, and from the various other planes to form life and the vehicles of life, such as our corporeal bodies. This ongoing construction adds to the complexity of natural forces and fields interacting within the planet.

Lifeforms can actually create new planes. Usually this requires a hospitable host environment such as that of Earth, but there is no reason why intrepid lifeforms could not colonize the secondary planes of other planets within our solar system, if they have not already done so. All they require is a usable source of energy. One of the most elemental traits of life is that it can adapt itself to use virtually any type of energy.

Each plane is constructed of some common base energy. Ours is constructed of base atomical energy; others have their own base. All are materially based energies, but their differences enable the vast panorama of life and experience that is possible within the planet Earth to exist. Interactions between planes lock in most of the physical activity of each plane, but lifeforms, because of their self-directed activities, can learn to remake themselves. This enables them to move from plane to plane as suits their needs, allowing a lifeform evolved on one plane to eventually establish itself on another plane. It requires a host vehicle to do so. Sufficiently evolved, a lifeform can become a physical plane unto itself. Such entities represent the highest level of evolution within our level of universe. In the ever-expanding way of self-directed life, new frontiers are constantly being explored, colonized, and developed into suitable habitats for as many types of life as possible.

It happens that terrestrial earth is a particularly difficult habitat in which to evolve. This plane requires enormous expenditures of energy for the simplest biological processes. Consequently, evolution here is slow. It is not, however, so slow that any life-entity is restricted to evolving at the pace of biological evolution. Races and orders of life-entity evolve quickly through their host vehicles. Most come to this plane from very few others, then return there or to one or two other planes. These planes form a set of planes souls call the astral planes. Their base energies are astral energies, a family of stable energies that can be molded into useful vehicles.

The astral worlds support many soul-entities. The base substances of the astral planes are well suited to soul-entities because of similarities between astral energies and soul-energies. Many lifeforms on the astral planes follow a reincarnational cycle very similar to that of terrestrial earth. Most true apparitions—that is, sightings of entities from other worlds within our world—are from astral worlds or "bridges" between our world and the astral worlds.

It is possible for the human soul to travel to astral worlds, though only the Spirit can make such a journey during an incarnation. Typically, the base soul does its travelling in the discarnate state; in fact, if the soul leaves the body, the body dies. The soul "travels" by extending its being through nature. I know this is a vague statement, but it is about as accurate as the language permits. By "extend" I mean to project outwardly from the self to other aspects of nature, such as our atomical plane, our Afterlife, or any of the astral planes. By "being" I mean, of course, the self. And by "through nature" I mean a physical extension of self through elements of "not self", or environment. The soul can select which aspect of nature it wishes to travel through, whether time, space, or some element of another plane.

When the soul travels, it does so at a much greater speed than the speed of light, even when travelling through space. This is because it is not travelling in conventional propelled terms, as on a spacecraft. The soul travels at the speed of *thought*, which is very nearly instantaneous. The extension of self through space is based on physical principles that lie outside the known physics of our three-dimensional world. There are a number of circumstances in which this happens, one of them being astral projection from place to place on our plane. Another recurring example is that of people who see a loved one appear unexpectedly when the loved one is hundreds or thousands of miles away. They find out later that the appearance occurred at the very moment the loved one died or experienced an extreme crisis situation. Essentially, the vision is a projection of the life-entity through space, manifested in visible terms. Similarly, the soul can extend itself through time, forwards or backwards. It can thereby analyze events of its future as easily as memories of the past.

Once locked in an atomical organism, however, some of the soul's spacetime projection opportunities are lost—or at least curbed. By physically bonding with the atomical energy of the corporeal organism, the soul is restricted to that spacetime location. It accepts these limitations for the sake of gaining terrestrial evolutionary experiences. However, the result is that the base soul must surrender its most direct control over the entity to a surface consciousness that is organized as an interface mechanism between the base soul and the corporeal body. This surface consciousness is the mind, and is the organized awareness associated with the Spirit.

When the soul joins the flesh, the elements of the soul interact directly with the biological processes of the corporeal body. The evidence of this interaction is apparent through psychomotor functions, brain waves, psychosomatic illnesses (and cures), the physical sensation of emotions (such as a "broken heart"), and other characteristics of our daily lives we take for granted. Thought, as mysterious as it is in its origins, is really the substance of the soul—specifically the mind, one aspect of the soul—at work. The in-flesh human being is essentially three living entities in one: the corporeal organism, the Spirit, and the base soul.

The organic body imposes certain limitations on the soul. The soul cannot zip off to Jupiter as readily as it would if it were discarnate. However, it can send its personal emissary in its place—the consciousness of the Spirit. This is astral projection, and although it is a substantially different process, it offers some insight into what happens at death. The Spirit leaving the body for astral projection may share many of the experiences that can occur at death. The key difference is that in astral projection, the Spirit is assured a safe return, but only a few people are revived following the early stages of death, and none from the latter stages. When the base soul leaves the body, it cannot return. The bond is broken and the flesh dies. The near-death experiences now being discussed so extensively in medical science and psychiatry are the first stages of death. The Spirit leaves the body, but returns before the base soul leaves.

Normally, our contacts with other planes occur at base levels of consciousness. This is the result of the base soul's awareness only being indirectly accessible to the mind. Our consciousness has evolved to the point where the mind in its natural waking state rarely has any conscious appreciation for nearby planes and the lifeforms therein. This is regrettable in many ways, because although biological survival dictates a need to focus on this world during terrestrial life, it is more recent cultural developments that separate us from any true appreciation of other planes and the lifeforms therein. In aboriginal societies, people are very much aware of nearby worlds. Perhaps their interactions with these worlds seem crude to us, but often that crudeness is more the result of our own crude perceptions. In fact, aboriginals are more fully aware of their place in not just this world, but the nearby worlds of unseen life. It just happens that in our industrialized cultures, we have allowed ourselves to believe we are fully self-supportive through mechanization. We no longer try to construct models of a universe that allow unseen lifeforms to coexist with us; until such is proved to us in objective terms, we refuse to believe it. Yet evidence of these other worlds creeps nightly into our minds, as our dreams are filled with entities that show up in our legends, myths, religions, and fairytales, but not our scientific paradigms.

This is our loss. For it means we have so little appreciation of our place in our universe that we cannot extend our consciousness beyond atomical earth. Aboriginals realize they do not have to have common purpose with another lifeform to join with it in a reverence for All that Is. They recognize that each of us is a part of a harmonious whole, in which many forms of potential experience may occur without ever being understood. If we could only capture some of that openness of mind we could probably discover in scientific terms the parallel worlds that mystic primitives happily accept. We must realize that while we are currently joined in a single pursuit, the evolution of the Human Race, each soul among us will someday grow out of this race and join a higher world. When this happens, we must choose between several potential experiences, and the atomical plane will eventually become just a place of memory, one of a number of planes of past experience. Perhaps in time we will learn to appreciate what seems so natural to aboriginal human cultures close to the earth; perhaps in time we will know in our minds as much of our place in the universe as our base souls do now. When we do, we will have an understanding of what souls call our Karmic Place.

Chapter Fourteen
MAN'S KARMIC PLACE

Man's quest is a quest for knowledge. The specific knowledge we seek most of all is knowledge of our place. At all levels, we seek to understand our position in the universe. This quest must be resolved to some degree within each of us. Without it, we lack that crucial sense of harmony with our environment that allows us to ignore issues of survival and get on with other tasks. The sense needn't be definitive; it only needs to be complete enough to satisfy the individual. In a baby, this sense may be provided by the presence of his mother. A primitive culture may find it in its mythologies or religious beliefs. Modern man finds it in science. Intriguingly, the motivation of a scientist to integrate his understanding of his environment is no less primal than that of the newborn child or the primitive.

Our sense of place is so important to us that it drives most of our learning experiences. We explore outwards from our selves to develop a sense of harmony with our environment. Much of our inner stress arises from our need to survive, which we seek to offset through understanding and mastery of our environment. As biological organisms, this need is inevitably thwarted at some point; we all must die. But as soul-entities, we do survive, and our unconscious recognition of this fact frees us from immediate concerns for survival to study our environment. In our most immediate context, this means learning about the atomical plane and how it affects us. How we learn may be the meticulous approach of the scientist, or more metaphysical, as exhibited by a primitive hunter-gatherer. Either way, the individual is motivated by a need to learn of his environment, for that environment determines what he is. Control of his destiny lies in that knowledge.

We all need to understand our place, and are each compelled to view the universe from our unique perspectives. Each of us believes our impressions of nature to be sound; in fact, primitives are as inclined to scoff at the beliefs of scientists as scientists are to scoff at theirs. Both have their own context and these contexts are closer than either would care to imagine. Although we are all part of the human quest, each one of us must individualize it according to personal beliefs and circumstances.

In science-driven Western cultures, we deem it important to understand our relationship with the universe in objective terms. We are somewhat betrayed, however, by our own nature. The universe does not allow us to be unbiased, no matter how much we strive to be. Our place is determined not just by where we are in terms of physical coordinates, but in how we *view* our position. We are as much the product of our own perceptions as we are the product of external physical forces. This unique combination of physical position and personal point of view is our personal locus of experience within the universal context. Souls call this personalized place for the individual or society a Karmic place.

Karma is an ancient concept familiar to us through Eastern mysticism. To souls the concept is a product of life itself. Karma, in the broader context of the soul's understanding, is the natural relationship of a lifeform with its environment as well as its self. Karma implies that there is order in the interaction between self and nonself, and that this order can be defined in stated truths. An individual has his own personal Karma, a population has a collective Karma, and even a world has Karma, both in physical terms and in terms of the entities living in it. To understand our own personal Karma, we must also know the Karma of our societies and our world. This Karma extends to our relationship with other worlds, other places in time, and interrelationships throughout nature we don't understand and have little hope of ever understanding. Karma is everything about us, shared with our unique place.

Karma is no simple subject. It is as complicated and as involved as the universe itself. An individual's Karma is his context of action and reaction, in effect the entire universe. Karma, therefore, is a personalized or subjective view of the universe, as opposed to some objective view. In the end, we all hold very subjective views of the universe, and objective knowledge remains an ideal. Our only truly objective knowledge lies in the mathematical abstractions of physical laws we have discovered. When we state a law, such as Einstein's $E=mc^2$, we are stating a truth as objectively as humanly possible. Yet we still view and interpret all such laws from a peculiarly human perspective. Our only unbiased certainty is this: we have a place in the physical scheme of existence which gives us our being. From that single awareness we build our world view. Though our world view may be mistaken in many ways, we can be assured that our place is perfectly defined by all that surrounds us.

This is not to say that objectivity has no place in man's quest. Any effort to objectify a piece of information or knowledge makes it that much easier to transmit to others. Communication is a valuable end in itself, even if our attempts to objectify knowledge fall short of our ideals. By reducing a concept, even a concept perceived only from the human perspective, to a mathematical formula, the concept can be passed on to others in a less biased form. Let's say Einstein attempted to pass on his views of relativity without heed to objective verification. Those views would then only be opinion subject to dispute by anyone. With the aid of mathematics and a foundation of observed phenomena, the subjectivity of the ideas is lessened. Einstein used known facts, observed phenomena, and precise mathematics to express his ideas. His ideas therefore retain a great deal of credibility, though they also remain open to much human interpretation. The ideas are specifically related to the human perspective of the universe— a relative viewpoint, if you will.

Westerners tend not to think in terms of Karma, preferring other terms that mean much the same thing. We think in terms of "our station in life", "achieving goals", "luck", and "fate", all terms that express aspects of Karma. However, it is more effective to consider our circumstances holistically, that is to say, in terms of Karma. We can rise above our station in life, be more or less successful, change our luck, or even bypass our fate by applying ourselves thoughtfully within our context. This is the element of free will: we can actively decide when to take what actions, thereby changing our circumstances to some degree. Naturally, there are many things we cannot change in the short term; this can lead to a passive interpretation of Karma, as in Eastern philosophies. In fact, we can change very little about our true selves in the short term. Major changes occur only after long preparation. In human terms, this means over many incarnations.

Karma evolves with the changing conditions of the entity. As you change your circumstances, you change your Karma. In fact, Karma realigns itself at each moment of existence (defining a moment here as a snapshot of physical reality which has no duration in time). If you bat a ball, the elements of your environment change at that moment in relation to that event. How great is the impact of any act depends on not just the act itself, but on what has led to the act. A hit or miss at a critical point in a championship baseball game has far more impact on the batter's life than a similar hit or miss in batting practice. It also affects many others: teammates, the opposing pitcher, the various team managers and coaches, the fans, and so on. A single event is the culmination of a vast history: years of training, dedication and development of skills on the part of the individual, and an impossibly complex set of external forces. No one event makes a great ball player, yet a single event can mark a turning point of a ball season, a team's fortunes, or a career.

Fate is perhaps the Western-oriented term most closely related to Karma, though it is unnecessarily defeatist. We are fated to be as we are because forces have combined to make us as we are; what's done is done. On the other hand, the situation isn't hopeless. Change occurs as of the present moment and we can begin to change our future by setting wheels in motion now. The elements of choice and free will lie in finding what aspects of our selves and environment can be changed in the short term and what can't. This process of definition is the daily decision-making process. At each moment, we are consciously and unconsciously making decisions. Each decision to act or not act influences the future by the subsequent events caused or not caused. In essence, Karma is the sum total of all events and nonevents as they relate to the subject, whether the subject is a single human or the entire species.

Karma is the sum total of every possible influence acting on a given moment, from a particular point of view. Man's Karma is to be a part of this planet, this solar system, and this cosmos, and he can do little to change that. A set of events has already caused him to be a part of that cosmic arrangement. Likewise, our soul-race has evolved into its current state; our Karma now dictates that we use the biological species man until we can collectively evolve beyond this need. This evolution requires development both in terms of intangibles, such as learning experiences, and tangibles, such as changes and growth in each soul of our race. The soul is where the tangible and intangible meet.

Physical events are integrated into the subjects's Karma; they are inseparable. In fact, the physical events of consciousness are very little different than any nonliving physical event. A decision of when and how to swing at a pitch largely determines whether the hit is a good or a poor one. Once the consciousness has decided to act, the physical events put in motion are largely predetermined. Part of being a good pitcher is knowing the batter's strengths, weaknesses and inclinations. To change one's Karma is largely (if not entirely) a matter of learning how best to deal with the physical environment, peers, and so on to achieve a desired goal. When life pitches a curve, you have to adapt your swing to stay in the game.

Karma includes both the internal and external forces acting on the individual or society. It is determined by past and present actions, and, in a way we can't understand from our linear view of time, the future as well. In the atomical plane, Karma is expressed through time and space; in other systems, Karma is expressed in terms coherent with their internal matrixes. Karma is an expression of self within a context, defining the entity within its environment.

Man's Karmic place, we must conclude, is what we Westerners would like to call his *real* place. Although the universe deals sparingly in absolutes, there is a great desire in the collective consciousness of the Western world to separate the *real* from the *unreal*. The Western practice—or ideal, at least—is to define facts as objectively as possible in an attempt to pinpoint our real place in the universe. Alas, this sense of reality is a bit of an illusion, though it holds more than a spark of truth. Although Einstein described a slightly more "real" universe than did Newton or Galileo, he did not tie off all the loose ends. Quantum theories bring additional reality to our world view, but at the same time have brought to light new loose ends. Even so, the scientist's idea of our place in a "real" universe is one and the same as the soul's idea of Karmic place.

We learn about the physical environment and our place in it whether we seek to change it or not. We constantly decide to act and not act, our decisions often made with little thought. In fact, we automate many of our interactions with our environment so that we are not even intellectually conscious of them. Such learning is a part of human nature, and a part of the nature of life in general. We build our awareness through action and reaction, the principle forces of Karma. Each movement, thought, and decision is a focus of our individual and collective Karma, an expression of what and where we are in the universe. Our actions are responses to our environment, whether we are conscious of them or not. We may or may not be conscious of scratching a slight itch, or we may forget a nagging headache when told that our favorite ballplayer has hit a record-breaking home run. Each time we act, we are responding to Karma. Karma has placed us in a particular context, that context being our lives and our universe.

For practicality's sake, we necessarily focus our specific perceptions to close out much of the overwhelming amount of data our environment throws at us. We cannot be aware of or intellectually analyze the whole universe at every waking moment. We therefore exclude most Karmic influences from our immediate perceptions. This applies both to events and physical nature. When in flesh, we tend to concentrate on atomical nature; when discarnate, we tend to concentrate on the noncorporeal nature of the Afterlife. In both contexts, we may ignore other planes altogether. The interests expressed are not just biases imposed by the environments themselves, but by the individual acting within the environments. In total, however, these two planes are just two major elements of our human Karma.

Man's Karmic place includes everything in his experience, his total biological evolution, and the histories of each soul and soul-race that has had a formative influence on this species. It includes all the experiences of all human beings currently on the face of the earth, and the total memories of every soul in the Human Race, in flesh and out. More, understanding man's Karmic place requires knowing the unknown, exploring the effects that the physical universe has on each and every one of us, however far afield that takes us. Obviously, such a task is an endless one, and can't be covered in a small book such as this. However, I can point to some of the major influences in man's Karma, starting close to home.

Let's consider the human point of view. Our planet is not a major element of the universe, we are forced to admit, but it is very precious to us. Without it, our evolution would take a radical twist, to say the least. Our biological bodies would immediately die; as souls, we would be locked in the Afterlife until we found other compatible evolutionary accommodations. Failing to do so would mean that we would eventually cease to exist as organized lifeforms—total death, if you will. But the planet does serve our needs, and provides us with a place to live, grow, and evolve. It serves the needs of our souls, and can be quite pleasant in many ways.

From the soul's point of view, the Karmic place of man is much broader than this plane. The Afterlife is equally important, though it has a different role. Its role is to provide a forum for rest and consolidation of experiences and self. To distinguish between the discarnate and incarnate orientation, souls often refer to terrestrial earth as "man's world", and to the soul's own vantage point in the Afterlife as a "soul-world". Other planes in which related souls dwell can also be referred to as soul-worlds, though they are also termed "astral worlds" because of the predominant matter-energies there. Worlds, to the soul, are defined more by perception than physical boundaries; the world of a hawk will differ from that of the mouse, though both may share parts of the other's world.

The major differences between life on this plane and life on higher planes are those that arise from adapting to their different primary energies. Whereas our corporeal organisms are constructed of atomical energies, the vehicles used by souls of other planes are constructed of the base materials of their respective planes. Despite common aspects between many souls of higher planes and ourselves, the differences of our respective worlds ensure that our circumstances and ways of life are substantially different.

However, we can be certain that we share certain ideals. The pains taken by our guides to teach us the higher ideals of our world indicate that they share visions of these same ideals. There are indeed striking differences in application and interpretation of ideals in their worlds and ours, but the essence of the ideals is the same. Love is by far the highest of these ideals. This ideal, say my guides, is the fundamental purpose of our learning experience on this plane. Of all the ideals we learn—freedom, justice, honor, and many others—love is the most basic to our existence. It relates to the essence of our being and is the governing factor in when and under what circumstances we, as souls, evolve to a higher plane.

The pursuit of ideals measures our progress in relation to other soul-entities; the pursuit of knowledge of self and environment measures our interest in our existence. We can say the human being is a focused expression of a parallel quest: the quest for knowledge always paralleling our quest for higher ideals. Whereas our highest ideals have been formed in spiritual philosophies, our greatest knowledge has come from science. These two quests cannot progress healthily if separate, as they often are today. One must counterbalance the other. Society stagnates without new knowledge and change; spiritual paths become meaningless rituals practiced by rote, and at times dangerous, as during the Inquisitions and witch-burnings of Christianity a few centuries ago. Conversely, science without conscience results in horrors such as Hiroshima. The integration of these quests begins with an understanding of the soul and its environment. By recognizing our spiritual paths as paths to higher materiality, we may be able to inject more spiritualism and conscience into our scientific pursuits. When science finally does reach out to higher planes, let us pray that our collective consciences are more developed than they are now.

Our lives are fragmented between our two major world views, that of the soul and that of our terrestrial incarnations. Naturally, this means we only experience at any given time incomplete perceptions of our place in life. In flesh, we see only our immediate reality, that of the atomical plane, and then only as well as our corporeal senses and interpretive minds allow. We see nothing or very little of other planes, including entities therein who try to contact us. Though they are real, we have no idea of how we affect them, nor they us. Worlds external to ours are just as important as this one, but we have not even the most elementary means of measuring interactions between planes.

What occurs within each plane forms first and foremost a chain of events within that plane, but at the same time can affect other planes quite directly. A soul passing from the flesh to the Afterlife and on to yet another plane is just a single example. The soul in this case is not so much travelling as an atomical body travels through space as refocusing its awareness. Its energy is capable of making such a transformation with relative ease; meanwhile, the atomical matter that composed the flesh of the biological organism is left behind. It decomposes because there is no longer the living energy of the soul to sustain it. Yet the experiences sustained in that flesh survive and are carried to another world, where a new set of actions will unfold, based largely on those prior experiences. This is only one way our actions live on to affect other worlds. There are many other interactions of physical energies; if our souls can pass across the barriers between planes, so can other effects.

Crossing over from our plane to the Afterlife (or any other plane, for that matter) involves crossing a field of energy. Normally, the souls of the Afterlife interact with their world with little impact on ours. Yet they can communicate with us, influence our lives, and cause physical reactions by encouraging us to certain behavior. Similarly, lifeforms on other worlds can affect our world. Of course, the crossovers occur in both directions, as at death and reincarnation.

The bonds between physical planes are real. They present barriers to the material that exists within each plane, and only certain configurations of substances can pass easily from plane to plane. Remember that all substances are configurations of the universal force, and the conditions of any configuration hinge on specific interrelationships. Certain configurations can allow a certain behavior while effectively blocking others. In any physical relationship, the prevailing conditions are all-important.

In our world, the prevailing conditions are those of the atom. Atomical bodies form our plane and govern the specific sorts of thing that can happen in this plane. At the same time, there are elements of nature that can superimpose themselves on this atomical nature while not necessarily interfering with atoms. In one sense, the soul is such an element, but it can and does interfere with atoms when it chooses, and when required to do so by nature. By joining flesh, the soul is interacting directly with atomical nature; the organism of life-supporting molecules is then directed by the living energy of the soul.

This interaction is derived from the respective worlds of the soul and the flesh. The interactions require that both the soul and the flesh shape each other. This effect extends to other planes because of how they depend on the atomical plane. For instance, our life-structure would conceivably be quite different if Earth were not located where it is in relation to the sun. If its orbital course were different, the entire planet would be different. Farther from the sun, no biological life as we know it could survive. Closer, and all earth's water might boil away into space. The different physical nature of the terrestrial surface would have extensive impact on other planes as well, very dramatically altering their internal realities. Just one different external relationship, a different orbit, could have altered the entire evolutionary history of this planet.

Our biological species is the product of a long and very specific evolution. It has responded in the most exact ways to every external stimulus and event. Some events have had more impact than others and we can therefore trace the major elements in our evolution. Science has done just that. Although there are many fine points (and some not so fine) left to be worked out in the story of human biological evolution, the general trend of current evolutionary theory is sound. But there is a second branch of evolution that science has overlooked, and one that is greatly influential in our history. This is the history of the soul.

The soul, too, is a product of evolution, though an evolution of a different sort than that of the biological species. The soul evolves according to its own criteria, using a vehicle such as the species man only as long as the species provides for the soul's evolution. For the time being, our race of souls finds it useful to merge with a particular biological species. The success of this convergence is obvious; we have risen in a few tens of thousands of years from just another beast on the savannah to a dominant cultural force, building large and sophisticated civilizations. Unless we make the ultimate mistake and unleash our nuclear arms, or more likely still, destroy our environment with pollution, it looks as if man will be the dominant biological species for a long time to come.

The story of the evolution of the human soul is not the only such story. Any lifeform has its own history, both in terms of its corporeal vehicle and its life-entity. Each vehicle, no matter how simple or sophisticated, has certain specific advantages over all others. This may be hard for us to understand, but for some lifeforms amoeba are more useful vehicles than the cells of human bodies. Each lifeform uses what is most specifically useful to it among the available vehicles. If a life-entity is not directly compatible with a vehicle it requires, it adapts. The adaptation may take a while to be successful, but the lifeform takes as much time as it needs. Time, in evolutionary terms, means very little.

The lifeforms using a vehicle establish a course for the vehicle's evolution as well as their own life-entity evolution. In biological terms, variations in species are sometimes initiated by efforts of souls acting on the energy matter of the body. Lifeforms choose a vehicle that best serves their most immediate developmental needs, as well as positioning it favorably for future development. The opportunities presented by the available organisms and prevalent conditions of the incarnate world are what limit the available choices.

Although there is for any lifeform only a limited selection of vehicles to choose from, a particular lifeform—or soul-race, to bring the discussion closer to home—need not be restricted to only one type of vehicle for long. The souls of the Human Race, as the souls using the species man are termed, use just this one species. However, another soul-race may use the bodies of several closely related species at any one phase of its evolution. No life-entity depends forever on any one vehicle. All evolve from vehicle to vehicle as appropriate to their own individual needs. Our soul-race uses only this one species of man because there *is* only one species of man. Biological races pose no particular incompatibility to a single soul-race. This means, of course, that the soul that incarnates into a social group believing in White Supremacy may well reincarnate in the next life in the body of a black man to correct the previous imbalanced perspective.

Soul-races in our world are loosely coupled to biological orders, evolving through the orders according to specific patterns. A single soul, therefore, evolves through various orders over many years. The Human Race is the most evolved race using the organisms of this world, though it is not as evolved as many lifeforms on higher planes. Man's Karmic place is determined as much by his nature as a soul-entity as his nature as a biological entity.

Evolution of corporeal life is restricted to a single plane; evolution of the soul is not. The biological entity merely supports life, it does not create it. However, our particular corporeal experience has caused us to be somewhat blind to that fact. We believe that biological birth, for example, actually creates a new lifeform. This is only partially true. While it *does* result in a new human being, one who has never before walked the earth, a certain core of that individual's experience is present in the base soul, which has experienced many other lives. Also, the biological organism itself is a direct off-shoot of two cells created by the parents. Although we personally choose to see great individuality in each person, this is largely a preference of perception as much as actual fact.

Our particular human perspective is to see that living organisms, both from the plant and animal kingdoms, have distinct individuality.

Although cells may split, we consider each to have its own status as an entity. This is our preference, but it is equally correct to see that all life on our plane has stemmed from a single biological source and continues to *be* that same source throughout history. Each permutation, each biological innovation, and each new species is just one more inflection within a single evolving entity, an entity of all biological life in our terrestrial world. With a broader perspective, we could see a vast pool of life that spreads itself from plane to plane, breaking off minute bits of itself to begin whole new lines of evolution, each one a fragment of the source. We might even see, if we had the perspective of future eons of time, how these fragments may someday converge into some more distinct whole, reuniting themselves in their source.

In our planet, each lifeform is a fragment of living matter that grows. Once started, it evolves forever irrespective of the number or types of vehicles it uses. There is no guarantee that any particular smattering of living matter will ever be a part of the human race, or any other race or order, for that matter. Its evolution depends on where and how it came to be, and what avenues of evolution open from that point. Its Karma is to a large extent predetermined by its origins; it must move forward according to the conditions set for it by its initial Karmic place. Lifeforms, once begun to evolve, evolve at their own pace, within the context set for them by their evolving Karmic place. Although the origins of all human souls must have been similar (as we have all wound up in a similar place), our origins are not necessarily all the same. We could as well have had a number of origins, and at some point converged through common interests.

There are many types of soul-entity and other lifeforms in the various planes of this planet that have never experienced life as a human being and never will. Others have experienced a full range of experience within the human context and have moved on to higher worlds and higher races of soul. Still others are evolving towards being human souls. The direction each lifeform takes depends on its origins, experiences and, as it develops to a certain state, its interests.

The vehicles used by each lifeform are determined by their current place in evolution. Our soul-race now uses the species man because things have worked out this way. This soul-race has used many other vehicles in earlier stages of growth but could not be described then as "human" souls. As we evolve beyond the need for this species and this world, we will someday cease being part of the human race.

To understand more completely our Karmic place, we must redirect to some degree our current biases. This does not mean we should stop or diminish current scientific research, but rather expand it to include nonatomical facets of our existence. This means studying the soul and the world of the Afterlife. It also means attempting to discover the material base for other planes, where our guides dwell and where we will someday dwell.

Bias is enforced at every level of human experience. We begin assuming an outlook common to our indigenous community at birth, and even before. Our parents, teachers, and the educational tools of society (television, newspapers, oral instruction, and social interaction) all impress on us the favored outlook of our community. We are guided to certain arbitrary social biases as certainly as if those biases were required by physical forces of nature. We are trained in what to think, how to think, and sometimes when to think by a social structure that is very persuasive. Such bias is only unlearned through time, a very great deal of time.

This inborn bias speaks of a history of social indoctrination that is as ancient as the species itself. It is as much a part of the human Karmic place as is the soul or the biological entity. In fact, it is the product of a biological evolution, with each social convention having its roots in the biology of the human animal. Without hands, we could not clasp them in prayer. Without some desire to improve our station, born of our desire to survive in our home environment, we would not pray. And without some knowledge of what to pray to, there would be no point in praying. As we shall see, there is a great deal surrounding this Karmic place of man, this niche that we occupy in an atomical world but that is equally a part of soul-worlds. Any and every aspect affecting us contributes to our place, and not least of these are our guides.

The presence of these guides has often been the source of much mystery and speculation, yet our history of myth and religious conviction adds credence to the notion that some greater intelligence has long guided man. The knowledge we have of this intervention is for the most part locked in our religious beliefs, seldom open to secular examination. Yet to understand our human existence, we must understand more than our atomical environment. We must understand all the influencing factors and shaping forces of our lives. In this regard, our guides, mythologized, idolized and sometimes bastardized, have played a major role.

We should attend our mythology as carefully as we attend our sciences. True, we can trust science's accuracy more than that of mythology, mysticism, or any other intuitive process. Yet we cannot ignore that man is essentially an intuitive animal, that although we possess reason, reason is useless to us without intuition. We are engaged in a quest for truth and knowledge, and we are allowing our minds to be overrun by a fascination with technology. No science will ever throw open the doors to all of the universe, not physics, not psychology, not even metaphysics. No one discipline or pursuit can access all the truths of the universe. We shouldn't let our frailties of perception and opinion keep us from any truths, regardless of how we discover them.

Chapter Fifteen
THE SEARCH FOR KNOWLEDGE

Man is striving to understand his own being and his origins. We study our environment in quest of clues to our origins, hoping to find microbes on Mars and artificial radio signals from space to indicate that our existence is not just a cosmic accident. Our guides (and our lower levels of consciousness) have assured us for eons that we are not alone, but that does not satisfy us. We won't be content until we unravel every thread of the universe that we can grasp—nor should we.

Our vantage point is very specific. What we can view from here is very much determined by what we are, where we are, and how we came to be as we are. We cannot yet hope to uncover the essence of the universal force, but we can explore and understand the base substances of our own level of universe. More specifically, we can discover the elements of life, much as we discovered the atomical elements. Life and atoms are both constructed of the universal energy; further, they are constructed of base matter energy. The interesting thing is how the characteristics of such constructions differ.

Life is not dependent on space. Atoms, however, are. There lies the greatest clue to the nature of our existence. In some way, life uses space to overcome certain limitations of its own nature. Our universal level is filled with lifeforms that never incarnate on this plane, but are similar in many integral ways to our own life force. Our planet is potentially only one amidst vast numbers of populated planets. But even if there were no other planets populated with atomical organisms such as ours, there would still be much life in the universe.

The forces that created life were generated long before Earth, as a planet, existed. The lifeforms here are the offspring, in a sense, of more sophisticated beings that evolved long ago. As this planet developed into a useful vehicle for life, life began to colonize it, plane by plane. Now, life has evolved to the point at which it can expand the number and nature of Earth's planes. Part of this effort is colonizing the atomical plane, introducing here principles of life already known to other planes. Undoubtedly, a similar process is occurring on other habitable planets within our atomical plane. The galaxies are teeming with life, the more gifted of which have already tapped the principles of inter-galactic travel.

The reasons why life uses this world can be understood in very simple terms. Life exists where it is possible for life to exist. Wherever a foothold can be gained, biosystems of incredible diversity can develop. In our world, biosystems of varying complexity have formed wherever sufficient energy exists in usable form. There is life clustered around hot vents in the ocean floor, miles below the surface. Single-celled lifeforms survive in the highest atmosphere, carried aloft by the winds. Strong wings carry certain birds, such as geese, thousands of feet into the air to suit their purposes of migration. In the coldest of arctic regions, life struggles to catch hold and live through the brief summers, or adapts to the cold waters under the ice. Wherever there is energy in an exploitable form, some form of life will sooner or later adapt to it as an environment and thereby open the door for more sophisticated lifeforms to follow.

In our world, life is dependent on the sun as the ultimate energy source. Green plants use sunlight in photosynthesis to create organic compounds. Animals—and other plants, such as fungi—then consume the plant's compounds and convert them into their own compounds. The food chain grows more complex as animals (and certain plants) evolve to eat animals. The trend of any food chain is to become more complex, evolving quite sophisticated intertwinings even in the most hostile of environments. There are food chains on glaciers based on bacteria that can live on snow; the bacteria feed insects that feed birds. In the deep ocean vents, chemosynthesis—the conversion of chemical energy from inside the earth into biomass, as opposed to photosynthesis, which is the conversion of light-energy from the sun—is the base of a food chain that supports many crustaceans. Life, once it takes hold, adapts to every nook and cranny of an environment to derive the greatest possible living experience.

To survive, we have to be aware of our place in our ecosystem. We are part of a food chain that depends as much on microorganisms as vast prairies of wheat. We have to be aware that each change we make in our environment has repercussions that can afflict us in terrible ways. Everything we do is absorbed in the perfect ledger of the universe. Each action has its endless reactions as the universe adjusts itself to what we do. The harmony of the universe must assert itself, and it does so as easily to our detriment or demise as to our benefit.

Within our world, we are supreme. We do as we want because we have the power to do so. Yet we often fail to wield that power wisely. We destroy our environment readily for short-term gain, and wage wars for causes often forgotten in the heat of battle. We wield our power injudiciously when it serves human purpose and hold it as our right to do so. In seeing our power in our tiny world, we forget how insubstantial that power is in the face of an enormous universe that doesn't always forgive mistakes. We forget to be humble. We must realize, however, that this world and everything in it can be changed—our oblivion is not obliteration, but a change of state so that man no longer exists.

Wisdom can change our ways. And as wisdom ultimately has but one source, we can find that source in virtually any direction we turn. That source is the universal force, a single thread we have in common with all that exists and that stitches us into the fabric of the universe. When the ancients speak of a single source, or of the one Truth, they speak of the universal force. This is the origin. Whatever we gain from an experience, it is a reflection of the source. Whatever we become, we become more of the source, and closer to the source. It is a mystic truth to understand oneness with the source, and a religious truth. What we don't understand in this world is that it is also a scientific truth.

Science is leading us through the maze of particles which constitute our foremost environment. Each equation and principle that we discover and enshrine in mathematics maps just a little bit more of the total universe. Our map is still woefully incomplete, but is impressive nonetheless. Beginning on the surface of this one atomical orb, we have mapped our world, our skies, and the major patterns of atomical matter. We have used powers of observation and intuition to discover mathematical principles that enable us to measure the distance between the earth and far galaxies—perhaps even to the edge of space. Each discovery teaches us a little more of the infinity of the universe, and each should make us just a little more humble.

We view our environment as we do because of our locus in space and time. We should never forget that we have ingrained biases simply because of what we can perceive. If we perceive only the cosmos, we leap to the conclusion that the cosmos is all that exists. Before telescopes, many primitives believed the sky was covered as if by a blanket. Stars were thought to be light shining through pinholes made by the gods. Science has brought us forward from such intuitive ideas, but must take us further yet. We now know the sky is covered by space, but still don't know what lies beyond space. When we view the cosmos now with our telescopes, we are emerging from a cloistered awareness, as if stepping out of an eggshell into a dimly lit room. It will be some time before we emerge from the room into the daylight to gain a larger perspective of our true environment; and never will we see it all.

Although our species dates back only some tens of thousands of years, the entire evolution of the cosmos has served to shape us. This is not to say that the cosmos exists for us and us only, but only that we are the product of cosmic evolution. This evolution is viewed from our peculiar place in space and time, concepts which are not as fixed as we would often like to think. Space we accept as existing all at once, though we see it as expanding. However, time also exists all at once.

Time is one of the cornerstones of our awareness of our selves and our environment. We peg our whole awareness to time, measuring every aspect of our reality from where we are. We identify that "where" as the present, keeping it carefully in place between past and future. And yet we know that time is a malleable quality. We know that it took billions of years to create the conditions of the cosmos that allowed man to evolve. What we don't know is what life would be like outside the framework of time. For example, we know that the atoms of the cosmos, including the organic bodies of any animals that may survive until then, will be destroyed if such a thing as the Big Crunch ever occurs. Will time stop then? Will it be temporarily suspended until the next Big Bang? Or will it carry on? And more important, can life, in any form, survive such a cosmic catastrophe?

Einstein was the first person to show us that time is not a constant, absolute force. As we go about our daily lives, any fluctuation in the passage of time is hidden from our notice. Such fluctuations are so minute that for our purposes they are negligible. Yet even though we attach no value in an everyday sense to such fluctuations, the universe tracks them as diligently as it does everything else. Our constancy is only a relative state, as Einstein might have said. Because of that relativity, time must be viewed in a manner as detached from everyday life as possible if we hope to understand it even a little.

Time is an integral aspect of the cosmos. It is not a fixed quality, because it does change in relation to the speed an object travels and the strength of gravity. However, it is a part of what comprises the cosmos. If space expands, that characteristic can only be measured if there is a quality of time that provides a measure for change. If there is a beginning and end to the cosmos, they can only be determined according to the passage of time between the two points. But these statements apply only to the cosmos as we understand it, not to the universe as a whole. The universe may indeed exist without time. If the cosmos ceases in the Big Crunch, there is no longer any space, gravity, atoms, or anything else that we associate with the cosmos. It is not unreasonable to hold that time, too, may cease to be. Time, therefore, is not a requisite of nature. Nature can and will endure if time is erased from being, just as nature can and will endure if humanity is erased from being. All we can be certain of is that if there is a change of universal state that erases time, human beings, or anything else, the substance or reality of whatever is erased will live on in some new form. An atom no longer an atom is some other form of energy; a cosmos no longer a cosmos also becomes something else. We just don't know what.

Perhaps one way to come to grips with these concepts is to adopt the same fluidity of mind the young Einstein used when he devised his theories of relativity. He at first could not fathom how the speed of light could appear constant from objects travelling at different speeds. In Newtonian terms, when one object travels 10 miles per hour, and a second at 20 miles per hour, their speed relative to each other is either 10 miles per hour or 30, depending on whether they are moving in the same or opposite directions. Yet that is not the case with the speed of light. It travels at a constant 186,000 miles per hour, and you see it as moving the same speed, regardless of how fast you are travelling or in what direction. To solve this problem, Einstein decided that time itself must be the factor that varies. Suddenly, his theory worked. It has since been proved correct.

Although Einstein was the first to shake the usual perception of time, we still hold only a slightly modified view. We now admit that time can flow at different rates, and that it may even under extreme conditions stand still, such as during the Big Crunch or at the surface of a black hole. But we still view time as progressing from the past towards the future, with no turning backward or skipping forward over as-yet unexperienced time; the official view is that only the present moment and no other is truly accessible to us. But having personally experienced "skips" of time, seeing actual glimpses of my future, I'm inclined to believe that time holds a few surprises for us yet.

Time is not inviolate. Just as memory reaches into the past, prescient dreams and visions can reach into the future. This prescience is like a memory of tomorrow, before it is formed in our terms. This leads me to believe that time is not just a progression from past to future. Instead, it exists as a singularity, having no beginning and no end. This eliminates the question of what went before the beginning of time and what follows the end of time. There is only a unity of field, the singularity imposed by the universality of nature. As metaphysicians have long stated, all time is now.

Relativity is a principle that can be applied to all universal experience. As certain aspects of the universe change, other aspects must change in step with these changes. The universe is one big chain of reactions to infinite varieties of actions. At all times, laws of conservation apply; nothing is ever lost, but merely changes state. Any change can be represented by an equation with both sides perfectly balanced. Consider Einstein's famous equation for the conversion of mass to energy and energy to mass. It is stated with explicit eloquence— energy equals the speed of light squared, or $E = mc^2$—and captures an incredible change of state. It also shows that nothing is lost in even the most dramatic of changes. The conversion is perfect, as all natural equations are. Our talent as mathematicians is in *discovering* the natural equations of the universe. Like the universe itself, the equation is beautiful in its perfection: each side of the equation is in perfect balance with the other.

Balance is achieved by the actions of change. Each event is part of a universal struggle to achieve ultimate balance, when all aspects of the universe are in a form of universal stasis. This universal stasis is the point at which the universal force is at its simplest configuration. In a sense, the universal force at this point of balance has no configuration. It is perfectly uniform, unidimensional, and simple. And from it, all of the complex forms of nature emerge. The emergence of something complex from the ultimate in simplicity is a form of self-creation.

Like the cosmos oscillating through cycles of Big Bangs and Big Crunches, the universe has had infinite cycles of universal stasis and recreation. It is as if the universe devotes its entire being to creating complex forms only so that it may reduce them again to their simplest common denominator, then start the whole process over. What actually occurs during each incarnation of the universe, or each cycle, we can only surmise from what has occurred so far in *this* universal incarnation. From our point of view, the obvious starting place is our own existence.

It is possible in the broadest possible terms to both exist and not exist. We exist now because the universe is organized in such terms that make it possible to speak of "now" and "existence". Given a different organization, one without time, it may not be so self-contradictory to say something may both exist and not exist at the "same time". Time itself can both exist and not exist. There are many vast portions of the universe that are not yoked to time as we know it. It just happens that *our* portion of the universe *is* so yoked. It is up to us to understand or not to understand how reality can exist in a timeless state. But with or without our understanding, time is only as relevant as nature dictates.

Shifting our focus of concentration away from such concepts as space and time are difficult. We are forced by our own natures to view space and time as inexpendable: we could not exist as we do without either. This begs the fact, however, that if the universe suddenly reorganized itself so that space and time no longer existed, we would not exist either. We would change state, the energy comprising us being used by the universe in a new way according to the laws of conservation. Though the universal constant would endure, there would be no human beings.

Our existence is oriented to a very small fragment of the universe. We are as much a part of the universe as any molecule or energy field and are therefore as significant as any other part. Our significance, however, is based only on the fact that we are part of an active equation. We are necessary to the universe only because we are already a part of it. Even less flattering is that the universe would be just as perfect if we existed in an entirely different form, or if our atoms and energies were reduced to their primal, nonliving forms.

The existence of anything, whether man, molecule or energy, is only as significant as its impact on its surrounding environment. That environment is ultimately the entire universe. Every part is required to complete the whole; every part can be reshaped according to the forces at work on it at any given point. Thus, the universe forms a perfect equation. The total substance of the universe equals everything that exists, and everything that exists equals the total substance of the universe. This equation, we could say, is the fundamental law of existence.

Naturally, this law is not fully defined. There remains the question of *what* is all existence. This question is the hard one, for it means devoting one's entire future to defining the universe. In human terms, defining the universe is the same as defining the word infinity. Ultimately, it is meaningless, except in the general understanding that it continues forever in every imaginable way. However, it is possible to define parts of infinity, and parts of the universe, in very specific terms. This is the effort of science, and the fruit of our quest for knowledge.

As living beings, we each quest into the nature of existence because the quest sustains our awareness. In whatever form awareness comes, it eventually causes a preoccupation with the self. We need to define our environment because we need to define our selves—one can only be defined in relation to the other. The universe as a total unit has no beginning, no edges, no end, but in smaller portions, there are indeed beginnings, edges, and ends. These parameters are really changes in state, but serve to determine what part of the universe is you and what part of it is me. We may never directly encounter each other, but in certain small ways our interactions can be known. I may affect your life through this book, or you may affect mine by voting for the opposite candidate in an election or by helping to build my next car.

On a universal scale, your efforts and mine are puny indeed. They are not particularly significant in terms of the outcome of universal evolution, if indeed on a universal scale any one event can be deemed truly important. My efforts in writing this book may have some small influence in the lives of my readers, but the sum total of all the changes wrought by all the books ever written will have very little effect on the outcome of the universal evolution. Man has little control over how the universe will unfold.

To the universe, it is unimportant if one person lives or dies, or if even this entire world ends. What is important is that physical balance be achieved. If this world ends, what comprised this world must become something else. There must be a change of state. The universe is quite amoral. If we exist as lifeforms, we borrow our substance from nonliving forms. We construct complex molecules of hydrogen, oxygen, carbon, and many other elements into biological organisms. Through the energy of the living soul, these compounds are in turn imbued with life. Then, after an ever-so brief time in living harmony, the biological organism dies. The complex molecules break down into simpler forms. The flesh decomposes.

But the soul survives. It later joins another body, and yet another. In time, it ceases to use human flesh altogether. It uses some higher form of matter, organized to suit its more sophisticated needs. This process is evolution, and though it has a far greater impact on the environment over the centuries than does any single effort in flesh, even it is insignificant in light of the magnitude of universal forces. What we do, we do because we *can* do it. The changes we make in our environment are to suit us, not any superior force driving the universe. We forge our existence within the framework set by the universe, using what exists to fulfill goals we set for ourselves. But everything that we achieve is achievable only because of the forces of which we are a part.

Our self-interest serves our sense of purpose, and the quest for knowledge expands that purpose. We care where we came from and where we are going. We have achieved a degree of autonomy within the framework of the universe and we choose to enhance that autonomy. We thereby increase our influence on the environment, but are ultimately still a part of that very same environment. To survive, as we so evidently wish to do, we must take increasing responsibility for our influence on our environment, as well as increasing control.

Control evolves from knowledge. We are gradually coming to understand more and more about the effects of our actions. These effects will never be entirely under our control, but as we grow and evolve in knowledge, so will our abilities—and, I hope, our sense of responsibility. To some extent, we exhibit greed in our shortsightedness: what we fail to control, we don't have to accept responsibility for. It is easier to destroy than to build, and when our ultimate intent is to build, we must be careful how we proceed.

Modern man has amassed a remarkable amount of knowledge about his three-dimensional sphere and its principle particles. As we struggle to cope with this knowledge, we see how it can enhance our lives and how it puts the survival of our whole species at risk. When we tap the forces of the atom, we realize its destructive potential as well as its creative potential. It will be the same when we begin to tap the forces of other planes. It is crucial, therefore, that we develop our sense of responsibility as we grow in knowledge. The havoc we wreak may or may not be destined; but when the universe cares so little about the fate of one small species or soul-race, we must care for our existence, and that of our world.

The care and nurture of any lifeform is ultimately up to the lifeform itself. There are interrelationships between lifeforms that act for mutual benefit, but these are the results of cooperative self-interest. The essence of society is learning to live with one another for mutual benefit and survival. Deliberate social cooperation is enforced by the very nature of the universe.

The universe is such that it forces all aspects of its being to conform to the perfect equation of existence. Everything that exists must conform to agencies that govern its existence. These agencies are the physical laws of the universe, which souls call universal laws. Each law is specific to a purpose, acting as it must within the context set by all other laws. Laws are the expression of order within physical nature. If there was no gravity, the atomical plane would take on a significantly different configuration. The atmosphere of our planet would float away into space, the planets would cease to circle the sun, the galaxies would disintegrate. Gravity imposes order on the atomical plane—our cosmos—and other laws impose order on other portions of reality.

Laws can express progressively more complex forms of organized behavior. Our social interactions, for example, are as much the result of the fundamental order of the universe as is gravity. These interactions have only stepped higher up on a scale of autonomy within physical nature. Nature, in other words, has through its inherent principles allowed us a certain degree of self-control. But no matter how complex any aspect of nature gets, the unity of the universal force imposes perfection on every physical equation. This is not to say that our social institutions or behavior are perfect, but that nature ensures that we break no physical laws while exercising our limited self-control. If a murder is committed, the flaw is one of self-control, not physical nature. No matter what action is performed, nature ensures that each action is whole and complete in physical terms.

These are the conditions of our survival. Whatever forces led to our existence in our current state have also instilled in us the desire to continue, to survive. Quite apart from survival as a human race, we have a desire to survive as souls. In fact, were it not for the soul's survival of bodily death, it is not likely that so many of us could so stoically face death. Thus, like it or not, we are alive and will stay alive for a long time to come. Whether we enjoy our lives or bemoan them is our own choice. Our critical needs are fulfilled nonetheless.

To live is to grow. And in growing, we develop stronger and stronger need to enhance the lives we lead. We enhance our lives through understanding the elements that make living more rewarding, by seeking out the aspects of our immediate environment that please us. In this befuddling array of universal forces in which we live, one of the greatest challenges—and greatest enjoyments—is sorting out just what makes the universe work. From the vantage point of this one tiny world, we can reach into the heart of all existence and learn the secrets of universal order. This is no unique skill; we could do as much from any other point in the universe. The truly great thing is that we are able to appreciate it. This appreciation is one of the most marvellous manifestations of the infinite universe.